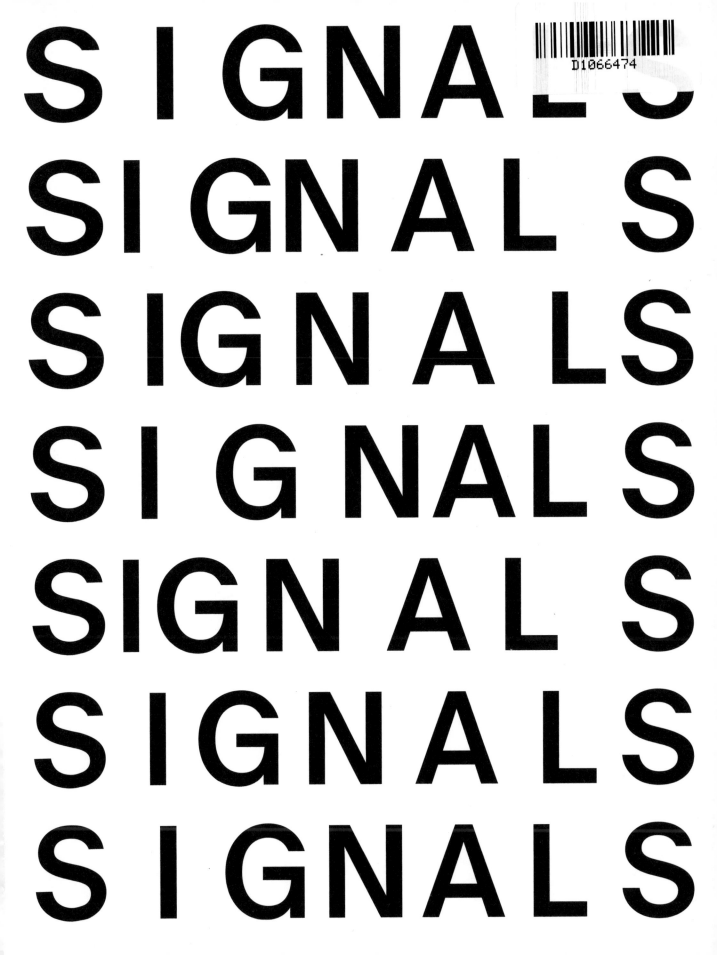

SIGNALS
How Video Transformed the World

Stuart Comer/Michelle Kuo

The Museum of Modern Art, New York

Passersby interact with *Hole in Space*, by Kit Galloway and Sherrie Rabinowitz, an unannounced telecollaborative public video/audio link connecting Los Angeles (left) and New York (right), November 11–13, 1980

Foreword

We have reached an unprecedented moment in the history of moving images, one in which the velocity and immediacy of their transmission across a vast international network of screens, platforms, and devices has shaped the "global village" first envisioned by Marshall McLuhan in 1962. This vast virtual public sphere has been marked as much by shock waves of disinformation and revolution as by the utopian ambition that first accompanied the emerging telecommunication technologies of the 1960s. Throughout the intervening six decades, and particularly since the advent of portable consumer electronics in the late 1960s, artists worldwide have used a broad range of tactics to engage video as a trenchant means of critique, reshaping the world through the very media that have absorbed us in endless streams of audiovisual information.

The Museum of Modern Art was an early champion of video art. Videos were first presented at MoMA in Pontus Hultén's 1968–69 exhibition *The Machine as Seen at the End of the Mechanical Age*, which featured works by Nam June Paik. In 1970, Kynaston McShine positioned this new technology as a global medium, including videos by artists from Latin America, Europe, Canada, and the United States in his landmark exhibition *Information*, a project that sought to examine "a culture that has been considerably altered by communications systems such as television and film, and by increased mobility," he wrote.

One year later, the Museum inaugurated its Projects exhibition series with a closed-circuit video installation by Keith Sonnier; this was followed, in 1974, by a new Projects: Video series. Continuing until 1981, Projects: Video presented some four hundred videotapes and ten installations by artists from eighteen countries. It became a key platform for Barbara London, a foundational curator in the nascent field of video. London also participated in "Open Circuits: An International Conference on the Future of Television," held at MoMA in January 1974. Gathering roughly forty artists, filmmakers, educators, administrators, critics, and television producers, the watershed event catalyzed a community and helped to secure a vibrant future for video at the Museum. The following year, London made MoMA's first video acquisitions, including works by Lynda Benglis and Joan Jonas.

These early acquisitions laid the groundwork for the distinguished media collection that now provides the material for *Signals: How Video Transformed the World*, an ambitious exhibition that reconfirms MoMA's singular commitment to collecting and preserving media art in its many and varied forms. The largest media exhibition at the Museum to date, *Signals* places recent practices in video—a fluid medium that continues to define how artists mediate politics and visual culture—in a profound dialogue with landmark early video experiments. The exhibition and catalogue highlight a technology that from its earliest moments was employed by artists to realize revolutionary dreams of transnational interconnection and to experiment with new ways of engaging urgent political developments closer to home. Detailing six decades of artistic practice, *Signals* is a manual for the present: it provides a critical lens for understanding a fractured but interdependent public sphere that is increasingly constructed—and taken apart—on-screen.

We are indebted to Stuart Comer, The Lonti Ebers Chief Curator of Media and Performance, and Michelle Kuo, The Marlene Hess Curator of Painting and Sculpture, who have assembled a topical and insightful framework for understanding video as a technology and a shape-shifting medium. They were supported by an outstanding curatorial team, including Erica Papernik-Shimizu, Associate Curator, Department of Media and Performance; Lina Kavaliunas, Curatorial Assistant, Piper Marshall, Exhibition Coordinator, and Eana Kim, Marica and Jan Vilcek Fellow, Department of Painting and Sculpture; and Rattanamol Singh Johal, Assistant Director, International Program.

We are enormously grateful for the generous support of Hyundai Card, which made this exhibition possible, and for the leadership support provided by the Jill and Peter Kraus Endowed Fund for Contemporary Exhibitions. Major funding for *Signals* was provided by The International Council of The Museum of Modern Art, the Wallis Annenberg Director's Fund for Innovation in Contemporary Art, and the Thomas H. Lee and Ann Tenenbaum Endowed Fund.

In closing, I extend my profound respect and gratitude to the artists in the exhibition, visionaries whose work defines the first chapters in the history of video, a technology that has reshaped artistic practice as rapidly as the world it reflects.

GLENN D. LOWRY
The David Rockefeller Director
The Museum of Modern Art

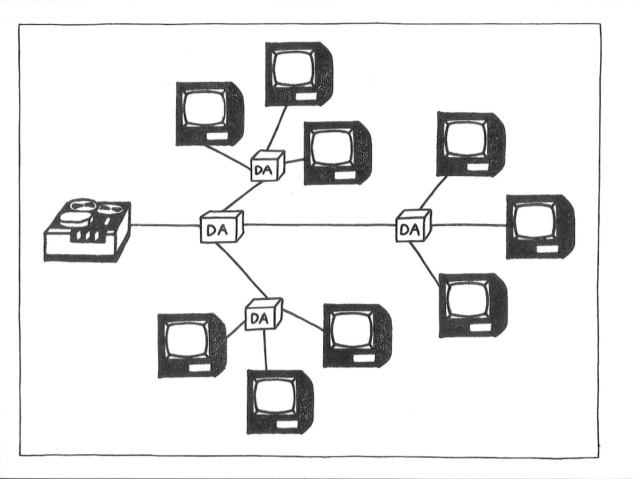

SIGNALS: HOW VIDEO TRANSFORMED THE WORLD
Michelle Kuo/Stuart Comer

Video is everywhere and nowhere at once. It surrounds us as signals and waves and data flows, but it remains ephemeral, shape-shifting, endlessly dispersed and dislocated. Unlike celluloid film, video can be instantly transmitted. And unlike traditional artistic materials, video depends on transmission: on destinations rather than origins, on simultaneous presence and absence, on images *here* relaying events *there* in an instant. Video became widely accessible as a consumer technology in the 1960s, but it also became subject to near-total corporate or governmental control in nations around the globe. Today it forms a pervasive and fluid media network that is thoroughly global, social, and interactive. Indeed, accelerated by the COVID-19 pandemic, video has arguably become *the* dominant mode of communication. Video is on our phones and our screens, shaping public opinion and creating new publics in turn, spreading memes and lies, evidence and fact, fervor and power, even stoking revolution. In other words, video is a means of politics and an agent of social change; it has transformed the world.

Artists have explored the social and political effects of video for decades, inventing tools, forms, and ideas in the process. Some hoped to create entirely new networks of communication, to stimulate democratic engagement and public participation. Others protested the rise of commercial and state control over communication, information, and life itself. *Signals: How Video Transformed the World* focuses on such investigations into video, art, and the public sphere. The exhibition is not a survey but a lens, reframing and revealing a history of massive shifts in society up to the present day.

Drawn from The Museum of Modern Art's important collection of video works—demonstrating MoMA's deep engagement with the format since the 1960s[1]—*Signals* features a transnational array of artworks that probe questions of information and disinformation, national and cultural difference, identity politics, economic access, and social inequality. The exhibition includes a number of large-scale installations that experiment with space and immersion in order to investigate contested landscapes and territories. In these works, video never sits still. It overflows boundaries of medium and geography; it splinters and migrates across varied viewing conditions, sites of display, and modes of address, from closed-circuit television to viral video, from private to public, from the Global South to the World Wide Web, from bodycam footage to "TikTok war," from agitation to persuasion to alternative facts. At a moment when media wield unprecedented influence, *Signals* poses video as an astonishingly prescient and vital current of art, one that has helped shape—and challenge—the networks of power within which we now live.

We normally think of politics as having to do with governments, territories, or military might. But at some point in the previous century, new communications media became extraordinary agents of politics, too. As the editors of the video-activist publication *Radical Software* declared in 1970, "Power is no longer measured in land, labor, or capital,

Opposite, top Diagram of a distribution amplifier network from *The Spaghetti City Video Manual: A Guide to Use, Repair, and Maintenance*, by Videofreex (New York: Praeger, 1973). Written by Parry Teasdale. Illustrated by Ann Woodward

Opposite, bottom A protester shares live video footage via the TwitCasting app, Rio de Janeiro, July 3, 2013. Photograph by Mídia NINJA

Radical Software 1, no. 1 (1970)

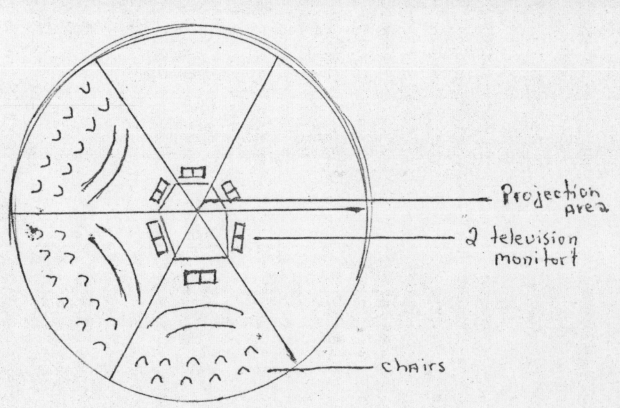

Illustration of Sputnik I,
the first Russian satellite

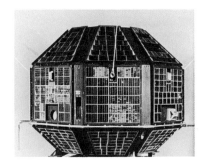

India's Aryabhata satellite

but by access to information and the means to disseminate it."[2] Around the world, the rise of broadcast television went hand in hand with nation building and new forms of political power, as scholar David Joselit has shown.[3] Mass media were inseparable from the consolidation of states and markets.[4] Telecommunications and research satellites—from Echo I in 1960 to Telstar in 1962, from Sputnik in 1957 to Aryabhata, the first Indian satellite, in 1975—were launched as avatars of the Cold War space race.[5] By the 1980s, these satellite systems became fully global in reach, opening up new channels for privatized media and local, small-scale networks in vastly different regions. Western media dominated international markets and served as a tool of globalization and cultural imperialism. But at the same time, alternative networks proliferated outside the West, whether the juggernaut broadcasting systems of post-Mao China or the local circulation of Aboriginal television productions in Australia. Communications networks were not uniform, smooth, or omnipotent but always fractured, dispersed, and multiple.[6] And audiences were never uniform, either. The cliché of the passive televisual spectator, the couch potato or the unwitting dupe, was, in fact, a cliché. Audiences—and artists—began to talk back.

To understand these forms of dissidence—of talking back—means understanding what audiences and artists were dissenting *from*. Most postwar histories set video art in opposition to television: "If anything has defined the formal and technical properties of the video medium, it is the television industry," David Antin famously wrote.[7] Video and television were locked in an antagonistic struggle. Corporate TV was video's "frightful parent" (Antin), "the most debased of our cultural conventions" (Douglas Crimp).[8] It was the totalitarian, top-down institution of social manipulation, chicanery, and kitsch that numbed citizens into apathetic, brainwashed automatons. Even Newton Minow, the chairman of the US Federal Communications Commission, famously dubbed television "a vast wasteland" in 1961.[9] To fight this broadcasting hegemon, artists and activists might use video against itself.[10]

For artists exploring video in this way, images were not enough. The televisual image was already shown to be unreliable, fake, simulated—a sham.[11] And so what was broadcast, or pictured, was not as important as challenging the broadcasting system altogether. The signal was a weapon. Regardless of subject matter, of representational content or depiction, the signal itself could be turned against the system, rerouted or reconfigured to create alternative systems of communication—or could even overthrow existing systems themselves.[12] As the artist Nam June Paik declared, "If revolution meant electrification for the Russians of 1920 . . . then revolution in 1960 means electronification."[13]

Such revolutionary dreams were in the air throughout the latter half of the twentieth century. In 1965 Stan VanDerBeek completed his extraordinary *Movie-Drome*: a spherical dome structure in which viewers could walk or sit or lie down while high-speed overlapping projections flooded the interior, enveloping viewers in a cascade of images of overwhelming "visual velocity," as the artist called it. But *Movie-Drome* was not meant to be an isolated event. It served as a prototype for a proposed global network of *Movie-Dromes*, all linked to orbiting satellites that could store and transmit images. Conceived as part of a worldwide communication system—a "culture intercom"—*Movie-Drome* seemed to affirm Marshall McLuhan's idea of a "global village" in which media technologies now allowed people to come together across vast distances, overcoming constraints of space and time.[14] Yet VanDerBeek also challenged the global village that already existed—the powerful

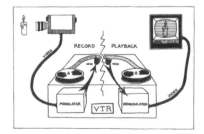

Stan VanDerBeek's *Movie-Drome*
at Design-In, Central Park,
New York, 1967

multinational networks of commercial television—and offered an alternative network, a new form of collective experience that occupied both
physical space and invisible airwaves, a counter–public sphere unlike
any the world had ever seen. This meant transforming television from
a top-down, one-way transmission system into a truly democratic network of multi-way feedback, communication, and exchange. Or, as
both John Cage and Paik had dreamed, a form of "electronic democracy through instant referendum."[15]

VanDerBeek was unable to realize his alternative network with
the tools he had at the time. Two years later, however, Sony released
its legendary Portapak—a portable, battery-powered video recorder
that was far less expensive than heavy studio equipment—effectively
making video far more widely available to consumers. The camera
was mainly targeted at Western markets, and artists in those regions
ecstatically embraced the technology. This newly accessible media
made early video art possible, with artists from Paik to Richard Serra to
Joan Jonas taking up the technology. Finally, it seemed, expensive and
enormous technological resources might be put into the hands of the
people. "Access to tools" was the motto of the *Whole Earth Catalog*, the
late-1960s counterculture publication that epitomized efforts to democ-
ratize technology and resources, and the Portapak radically advanced
this politics of redistribution.

Artists could record video on their own, but they couldn't always relay
its signals. Most video work in the 1960s was never broadcast because

Diagram showing recording and
playback with a video tape recorder
from *The Spaghetti City Video
Manual: A Guide to Use, Repair,
and Maintenance*, by Videofreex

Volume 2, Number 1 - $1.95

Front and back covers of
Radical Software 2, no. 1 (1972)

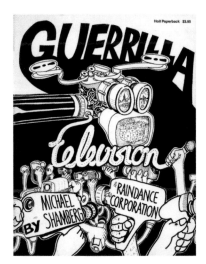

Guerrilla Television, by Michael Shamberg
and Raindance Corporation (New York:
Holt, Rinehart and Winston, 1971)

half-inch tape could not be transmitted. Some, however, broke through. In Buenos Aires in 1966, Marta Minujín broadcast her *Simultaneidad en simultaneidad* (*Simultaneity in Simultaneity*) on local television, a tactical insertion of an artistic Happening into mainstream channels. (An attempt to link to stations in Berlin and New York did not come to pass.) WGBH in Boston and other American public stations took part in the Artists-in-Television program, begun in 1967; that same year, the organization Experiments in Art and Technology, or E.A.T., proposed artists' residencies in television research at CBS and RCA; and Otto Piene and Aldo Tambellini launched their famous "Black Gate Cologne" broadcast on WDR (Westdeutscher Rundfunk) in Germany in 1968.[16] Throughout the next decade, "guerrilla television" and activist video exploded, with groups such as Raindance Corporation, TVTV (Top Value Television), Videofreex, Women's Television News Service, and Video Hiroba taking their Portapaks to the streets, broadcasting from political conventions and protests alike. These groups also envisioned a public use of cable television that opposed not only the "big three" American commercial networks but also the channels Sterling and Teleprompter in the US and Tokyo Cable Vision in Japan, exemplars of the reactionary commercialization or bureaucratization of cable. Their hopes for televisual democracy lay in disturbing the existing system from the outside—witness Videofreex's illegal, unlicensed, pirate television station, established in the Catskills in 1972 and the first of its kind in the US.[17] That same year, as outlined in an issue of the *Black Panther* newspaper, the Black Panther Party hoped to create an independent cable channel, formed through a "third world coalition" that would provide an insurgent, alternate network of connection and information.[18] Cable television and community-access television (CATV) promised a form of direct democracy for local audiences and experimental broadcasts. These tools might allow the development of a grassroots pirate media—a counter-public sphere, the "mythical public sphere of broadcast television."[19] The Portapak and CATV directly linked video to social change.[20]

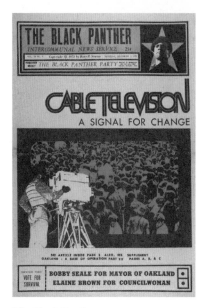

But video cannot simply be understood in opposition to commercial television. Video was not just TV's other. *Signals* aims to undo this long-standing binary, which has structured so many other exhibitions and histories of video.

    In the Western context of corporate broadcast television and advertising, television was about—or simply *was*—the commodity. "Television delivers people," as Richard Serra and Carlota Fay Schoolman noted in 1973, and audiences were always the most valuable product, both consumers and consumed. But in other realms, video was not about capital; it was about state power. The rise of state-run media in Egypt or Eastern Europe or China was often literally programmed by ministries of information rather than of culture, orchestrated by bureaucrats rather than CEOs.[21] These regimes attempted to forge new conceptions of citizenship and nationhood. And in the shadow of these state networks, the politics of video was not only about countercultural revolt or oppositional subjects but about creating new identities and subjects altogether. While American artists took up the Portapak as a tool of resistance against "Media-America," for instance, artists in other regions constructed wholly different kinds of "imagined communities" across disparate places and times.[22]

    In Japan, access to both tools and airtime was not widespread until the 1970s, despite the fact that Sony, maker of the Portapak, was headquartered there. The collective Video Hiroba, founded in 1972, created videos documenting everyday life in small communities that were rarely, if ever, addressed or covered by government media. Another group, Video Information Center, operated on a deliberately small scale to effect new kinds of media representation. Instead of using video to create an underground movement or network, Video Information Center wanted "to use video as a cultural tool to reach people on a more personal level," as the artist and Video Hiroba cofounder Fujiko Nakaya wrote.[23] Nakaya's own *Friends of Minamata Victims—Video Diary* (1972) captures a social environment in the wake of environmental disaster: the work is "a corporate indictment" of the Chisso Corporation, whose chemical plant in Minamata released wastewater that poisoned thousands of people; Nakaya created a montage from direct footage of protesters as they sought to agitate against the deadly crime.[24] She then played back the video to different shifts of protesters during the demonstration so they could communicate with each other. Decades later, in 1992, Harun Farocki and Andrei Ujică assembled *Videograms of a Revolution*—a media meditation on the Romanian Revolution, the turning point of which was the occupation of the state television station in Bucharest, when protesters broadcast continuously for 120 hours. Demonstrations and events were both made for state media and recorded by amateur videographers from the rooftops, overriding government censorship and introducing a constant stream of signals, of newfound visibility. "If at the outbreak of the uprising only one camera dared to record," noted Farocki, "hundreds were in operation on the following day."[25]

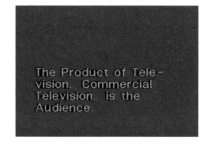

Video is not just about or against TV, then; it also confronts the surveillance state. The singular technology of the live signal, of simultaneous transmission—monitoring and being monitored—has formed the ground for some of the most powerful works since the inception of video. Many artists used closed-circuit television in the early days of the genre, and these works have largely been read as self-reflective, even solipsistic or narcissistic, examinations of the individual subject.[26] But closed-circuit—the real-time mechanical eye that takes in everything, unblinking—is also the basis of surveillance video. Michael Klier's *Der Riese* (*The Giant*) (1983) adopts this looming robovision, collecting material entirely recorded by remote-controlled surveillance cameras across Berlin. The work charts the increasing privatization and panoptics of public space—eroding the very definition of public space in the process.[27] Tony Cokes's *Black Celebration* (1988) comprises footage of the Watts riots and other flashpoints of racial and social unrest in the 1960s, overlaid with an industrial music track and pop lyrics appearing as text across the screen. The result is a kind of dystopian music video that refuses legibility and visibility, mounting a searing critique of modern Western capitalism as inseparable from anti-Blackness, as Aria Dean argues in these pages. In this way, the work presages the use of police bodycams and government surveillance to control and manage insurrection.[28] That Big Brother age has, of course, since come to pass, and Sondra Perry proposes ways of evading the all-seeing oculus of facial recognition and biometric control. Her *Double Quadruple Etcetera Etcetera I & II* (2013) is a training ground, an immersive field in which the artist repurposes Photoshop tools to render the Black subject dazzlingly spectacular and yet nearly invisible, dissolving or going underground, when doing so has become virtually impossible.

Video as active agent, video as passive recorder: each scenario has inaugurated novel forms and formats of social struggle. In the twenty-first century, a new generation of art and media collectives has coalesced in the wake of social media. Take, for example, the Mumbai-based duo CAMP, the Syrian collective Abounaddara, or the Brazilian collective Mídia NINJA, all of which practice factography in the age of Facebook, capturing direct phone-camera footage of protests, violence, and suppression in order to upload and share documentation of events not normally covered by mass media. These endeavors form local networks and micro-communities online, unexpectedly echoing Jaime Davidovich's countercultural public-access shows of the 1980s, or Ryan Trecartin's delirious YouTube subcultures from the early aughts. In our current moment, such diverse efforts to share information and create alternative public spheres may be seen in the frenetic TikTok videos documenting—and often agitating against—the Russian invasion of Ukraine. It is no coincidence that the artist Dana Kavelina's epic video-poem *Letter to a Turtledove* (2020) was originally meant to be released on YouTube, and incorporates footage from the anonymously authored online video *To Watch the War* (2018), which is composed of 422 video clips from the Russian invasion of the Donbas region of Ukraine. Kavelina has said, "These pieces of evidence were so compelling to me that I felt the need to create an additional space for dialogue between them—which, for me, is a dialogue between the past and present, between the political and the intimate."[29] The artist interlaced this found footage with archival footage of the Donbas region in the 1930s and '70s and with lyrical drawings, animations, and verse to create a collectively authored, polyphonic plea for peace.

Previous page

Top Hakudō Kobayashi, cofounder of Video Hiroba, conducts interviews in Tokyo, 1978

Bottom Visitors to *Video Communication: Do-It-Yourself Kit*, Tokyo, 1972

Tony Cokes. *Black Celebration*. 1988. Standard-definition video (black and white, sound), 17:11 min. The Museum of Modern Art, New York. Friends of Education and Committee on Media and Performance Funds

Sondra Perry. *Double Quadruple Etcetera Etcetera I & II*. 2013. Two-channel high-definition video (color, silent), 9 min. The Museum of Modern Art, New York. Acquired through the generosity of Lonti Ebers, Sarah Arison, The Lumpkin-Boccuzzi Family Collection, and The Modern Women's Fund

Dana Kavelina. *Letter to a Turtledove*. 2020. High-definition video (color, sound), 20:55 min. The Museum of Modern Art, New York. Acquired through the generosity of Bilge Ogut and Haro Cumbusyan

Michael Klier. *Der Riese* (*The Giant*). 1983. Standard-definition video (black and white and color, sound), 82 min. The Museum of Modern Art, New York. Committee on Media and Performance Funds

Tiffany Sia. *Never Rest/Unrest*. 2020. High-definition video (color, sound), 29 min. The Museum of Modern Art, New York. Fund for the Twenty-First Century

Like the chaotic and striated spaces of social media, the physical spaces of the built environment have become wildly heterogeneous terrains, or "mediascapes."[30] High-tech circuits of information may exist within decaying physical infrastructure, and small media, bootleg video, and VPN tunnels may infiltrate or evade state-sponsored networks—a condition that can be characterized as a kind of "pirate modernity," media theorist Ravi Sundaram has argued.[31] *Signals* stages a confrontation between these different registers of virtual and architectural experience. Artist Tiffany Sia's *Never Rest/Unrest* (2020) is presented on a monitor suspended from a horizontal bar structure in front of a floor-to-ceiling window, playing the aspect ratio of her work—shot on an iPhone—against the verticality of the Museum's architecture. Sia's experimental film presents an alternative, embedded reportage of the 2019 Hong Kong protests, its handheld, low-fi perspective evading state surveillance in a city quaking with tumult, suppression, and subterfuge. In *The Excluded. In a Moment of Danger* (2014), the Russian collective Chto Delat go so far as to construct their own quasi-architectural enclosure because, as dissidents, they have been excluded from public life, from public speech. "What remains of public space is disappearing before our eyes; and we have no levers of political influence. . . . Our voice is heard less and less, excluded and cut off from the chorus of voices," they intone. The installation surrounds viewers with videos featuring a polyvocal chorus based on the speeches of the Russian revolutionary Ippolit Myshkin. The work is both theater and refuge, information channel and seditious lament.

Writing now, in 2022, it seems as if all those revolutionary dreams of video—the participatory network, multi-way communication, the democratization and decentralization of information—have come to pass. Video as social media means an unprecedented proliferation of public spheres. But it also means the disintegration of those publics into niche audiences, the atomization of politics into a seemingly limitless series of echo chambers. Things haven't quite worked out the way we thought they would.[32] New forms of distribution and reproducibility inspire new forms of control, as scholar Erika Balsom has noted, and the decentralization of information has not led to the redistribution of power.[33] The top-down dissemination of information via mass culture in the twentieth century has instead been hyperdiversified, splintered. Talking back—feedback—has merely been assimilated back into the system, is in fact constitutive of the system: training it, regulating it, making it better, more efficient. Glitches are absorbed as soon as they arise. And, in turn, new voices of authoritarianism have learned to *overload* the system, to flood all signals with noise. Their rumble flows from the esoteric reaches of the internet and from the corridors of power; it cascades through the media apparatus and is amplified—exponentially, monstrously, virally. Fakes and leaks and fiction inundate the circuits. Video evidence is all too often drowned out. If we are to survive the noise, if we are to find new publics and politics and forms of communion amid the din, we might look to the artists in these pages. They have shown us, time and again, how to send a signal—and, perhaps, transform the world.

Ant Farm. *Media Burn*. 1975–2003. Standard-definition video (color, sound), 23:02 min. The Museum of Modern Art, New York. Acquired through the generosity of Celeste Bartos and as a gift of Chip Lord

1 MoMA's early video exhibitions and programming include *The Machine as Seen at the End of the Mechanical Age* (1968–69), *Information* (1970), "Open Circuits: An International Conference on the Future of Television" (1974), and *Video and Satellite* (1982). Curator Barbara London organized the latter and spearheaded the Museum's adoption, acquisition, and programming of video for decades.

2 Editorial, *Radical Software* 1, no. 1 (Summer 1970): 1. The pronouncement echoed the words of the renegade FCC commissioner Nicholas Johnson. See Johnson, *How to Talk Back to Your Television Set* (Boston: Little, Brown, 1970), 85.

3 When Eisenhower invented the TV news conference in 1955, David Joselit recounts, he bypassed "the role of the press as an interlocutor. . . . The explicit goal of his advisors was to deliver information directly from the president to the public via the edited film or transcription," selling a product "through mass communication to audiences that can't talk back." Because such access is enormously expensive, Joselit observes, "the televisualization of presidential politics constitutes a serious threat to democracy." Joselit, *Feedback: Television against Democracy* (Cambridge, MA: MIT Press, 2007), 139–41.

4 On the ways in which television perpetuated the "dominant codes" of the nation-state, see Stuart Hall, "Encoding and Decoding in the Television Discourse" (1973), in *Essential Essays*, vol. 1 (Durham, NC: Duke University Press, 2018). See also Raymond Williams, *Television: Technology and Cultural Form* (1974; London: Routledge, 2003).

5 Aryabhata, a collaboration with the USSR, was an important marker for the Non-Aligned Movement. See Asif Siddiqi, "Another Global History of Science: Making Space for India and China," *BJHS Themes* 1 (2016): 115–43.

6 See Jürgen Habermas, *The Theory of Communicative Action*, 2 vols., trans. Thomas McCarthy (Boston: Beacon, 1981–87); Oskar Negt and Alexander Kluge, *Public Sphere and Experience: Analysis of the Bourgeois and Proletarian Public Sphere* (1972; New York: Verso, 2016); William Kaizen, *Against Immediacy: Video Art and Media Populism* (Lebanon, NH: Dartmouth College Press, 2016); and Dara Birnbaum, "Talking Back to the Media" (1985), Tetsuo Kogawa, "Video: The Access Medium" (1996), and Ulrike Rosenbach, "Video as a Medium of Emancipation" (1982), in *Video Theories: A Transdisciplinary Reader,* ed. Dieter Daniels and Jan Thoben (New York: Bloomsbury Academic, 2022).

7 David Antin, "Television: Video's Frightful Parent," *Artforum* 14, no. 4 (December 1975): 36.

8 Antin, "Video's Frightful Parent"; Douglas Crimp, *Pictures: An Exhibition of the Work of Troy Brauntuch, Jack Goldstein, Sherrie Levine, Robert Longo, Philip Smith*, exh. cat. (New York: Artists Space, 1977), 28.

9 Newton Minow, "Television and the Public Interest," address to the National Association of Broadcasters, Washington, DC, May 9, 1961.

10 See Joselit, *Feedback*.

11 See Jean Baudrillard, *Simulacra and Simulation*, trans. Sheila Glaser (1981; Ann Arbor, MI: University of Michigan Press, 1995).

12 See Ina Blom, *The Autobiography of Video: The Life and Times of a Memory Technology* (London: Sternberg, 2016); and Joselit, *Feedback*.

13 Nam June Paik, interview by Jud Yalkut (1968), in *Modern Sculpture: Artists in Their Own Words*, ed. Douglas Dreishpoon (Berkeley: University of California Press, 2022), 185. On Paik's satellite art, including *Good Morning, Mr. Orwell* (1984), and the context for *Our World* (1967), the first live multinational multi-satellite broadcast, see Gregory Zinman, "'This Script Is Not Final, and Is Subject to Changes': Nam June Paik between Page and Screen," in *We Are in Open Circuits: Writings by Nam June Paik*, ed. John G. Hanhardt, Zinman, and Edith Decker-Phillips (Cambridge, MA: MIT Press, 2019), 73–85.

14 For "visual velocity" and "culture intercom," see Stan VanDerBeek, "Culture: Intercom and Expanded Cinema: A Proposal and Manifesto," *Film Culture*, no. 40 (1966): 15–18. See also Gloria Sutton, *The Experience Machine* (Cambridge, MA: MIT Press, 2015), and Erica Levin, *The Channeled Image* (University of Chicago Press, 2022).

15 John Cage, "Diary: How to Improve the World (You Will Only Make Matters Worse)" (1966), in *A Year from Monday: New Lectures and Writings* (Middletown, CT: Wesleyan University Press, 1967), 52; Nam June Paik, 1968–70 essay for MoMA's *The Machine as Seen at the End of the Mechanical Age*, expanded in *Nam June Paik: Videa 'n' Videology, 1959–1973*, ed. Judson Rosebush (Syracuse, NY: Everson Museum of Art, 1974).

16 On these early video art initiatives and their relationship to network television and electronic democracy, see "TV as a Creative Medium," exh. brochure (New York: Howard Wise Gallery, 1969); Joselit, *Feedback*; and Gregory Battcock, ed., *New Artists Video: A Critical Anthology* (New York: Dutton, 1978). For an exemplary statement of the conflicted artistic motivations for participating in the exhibition *TV as a Creative Medium*, see Paul Ryan, letter to Howard Wise, March 2, 1969, Paul Ryan Papers, 1943–2008, Archives of American Art, Smithsonian Institution. For the sociological dimensions of television networks in Europe, see Pierre Bourdieu, *On Television*, trans. Priscilla Parkhurst Ferguson (New York: New Press, 1998), 36–37.

17 See Parry D. Teasdale, *Videofreex: America's First Pirate TV Station and the Catskills Collective That Turned It On* (Hensonville, NY: Black Dome, 1999). On Raindance Corporation, its journal *Radical Software*, and CATV, see Joselit, *Feedback*, 85–132; Paul Ryan, "Cybernetic Guerrilla Warfare," *Radical Software* 1, no. 3 (Spring 1971): 1–2; and William Kaizen, "Steps to an Ecology of Communication: *Radical Software*, Dan Graham, and the Legacy of Gregory Bateson," *Art Journal* 67, no. 3 (Fall 2008): 86–106.

18 "Cable Television: A Signal for Change," *Black Panther*, December 7, 1972.

19 Benjamin H. D. Buchloh, "From Gadget Video to Agit Video: Some Notes on Four Recent Video Works," *Art Journal* 45, no. 3 (Fall 1985): 217.

20 Paul Ryan, "Genealogy of Video," *Leonardo* 21, no. 1 (1988): 39–44.

21 See Faye D. Ginsburg, Lila Abu-Lughod, and Brian Larkin, eds., *Media Worlds: Anthropology on New Terrain* (Berkeley: University of California Press, 2002).

22 See Michael Shamberg and Raindance Corporation, *Guerrilla Television* (New York: Holt, Rinehart and Winston, 1971) for "Media-America"; and Benedict Anderson, *Imagined Communities: Reflections on the Origin and Spread of Nationalism*, rev. ed. (1983; London: Verso, 2016).

23 Fujiko Nakaya, "Video of the Seventies in Japan," in *Video from Tokyo to Fukui and Kyoto*, ed. Barbara J. London (New York: The Museum of Modern Art, 1979), 11.

24 Nakaya, "Video of the Seventies," 22.

25 Harun Farocki, quoted in Dietrich Leder, "Videograms of a Revolution," on the artist's website, www.harunfarocki.de/films/1990s/1992/videograms-of-a-revolution.html. The work was first broadcast on West3 in Germany in 1993.

26 Rosalind Krauss, "Video: The Aesthetics of Narcissism," *October* 1 (Spring 1976): 50–64.

27 See Branden W. Joseph, "Nothing Special: Andy Warhol and the Rise of Surveillance," in *CTRL [SPACE]: Rhetorics of Surveillance from Bentham to Big Brother*, ed. Thomas Y. Levin, Ursula Frohne, and Peter Weibel (Cambridge, MA: MIT Press, 2002), 237–51.

28 See Giorgio Agamben, "Thought Is the Courage of Hopelessness," interview by Juliette Cerf, *Verso* (blog), June 17, 2014.

29 "Dana Kavelina in Conversation with Oleksiy Kuchanskyi," e-flux Video & Film (online), July 2020.

30 See Arjun Appadurai, ed., *The Social Life of Things: Commodities in Cultural Perspective* (Cambridge, UK: Cambridge University Press, 1986).

31 Ravi Sundaram, *Pirate Modernity: Delhi's Media Urbanism* (London: Routledge, 2009). See also "Pirate Media," by Sundaram, in this volume.

32 *Pace* Hans Magnus Enzensberger, "Constituents of a Theory of the Media," *New Left Review*, no. 64 (November/December 1970): 13–36. See also Irene Small, "Live Streaming," *Artforum* 52, no. 9 (May 2014): 286–90.

33 See Erika Balsom, *After Uniqueness: A History of Film and Video Art in Circulation* (New York: Columbia University Press, 2017).

TELEVISION AT THE END OF HISTORY
Erika Balsom

I

In the summer of 1989, on the eve of the Soviet Union's collapse, political scientist Francis Fukuyama wagered that the end of history had arrived. From then on, he proposed, economic and political liberalism would reign unchallenged. Fukuyama grounded his remarks in a scene of spectatorship: "In watching the flow of events over the past decade or so, it is hard to avoid the feeling that something very fundamental has happened in world history."[1] Perhaps the notion of watching a flow of events is nothing more than a metaphor; evaluating the role of media technologies is, after all, far from Fukuyama's concern.[2] Nonetheless, it is tempting to take his language as an invitation to consider the extent to which the fundamental shift in historical consciousness occurring at the time was inextricable from the sense that history could be *watched* in new ways. Television offered the possibility of witnessing history unfold in real time, transforming it into something to be consumed, something that poured out from screens in a seemingly endless, even flow—as if there were so much of it that there was none of it.

For film and television critic Serge Daney, 1989 was the year that television underwent its "baptism by fire" as a historical agent, decisively taking over from cinema as the medium tasked with rendering world events visible.[3] First there was Tiananmen Square, then the fall of the Berlin Wall. The defining moment, however, arrived in December, in Romania, with the overthrow of Nicolae Ceaușescu's dictatorship. On December 21, while protests continued in Timișoara, Ceaușescu held a mass rally in Bucharest, broadcast live. In video footage of the event, one can clearly see the moment when Ceaușescu's attention is stolen by a commotion in the crowd. He falls silent and the camera wobbles. The signal falters and the feed is cut, only to resume with the embattled leader looking rattled. Over the five tumultuous days that followed, the regime swiftly crumbled, its dissolution caught on tape by dozens of cameras, amateur and professional. This revolution *would* be televised, broadcast from the Romanian Television Center in Bucharest, where Studio 4 was occupied by revolutionary forces. On December 26, these transmissions culminated in a macabre spectacle: Nicolae and Elena Ceaușescu's execution by firing squad, taped the day before, beamed into homes for all to see.

Seizing the means of image production, turning television against repressive state power: the Romanian Revolution initially appears to have been a triumphal moment of democratic image politics—an event during which television served as a tool of counter-information and its capacity for liveness was marshaled in the service of emancipation. Yet, for Daney, writing just a few months later, in April 1990, the medium's reckoning with historical actuality in Romania resulted in merely a "Pyrrhic victory."[4] Images circulated widely of the bodies of those killed by the regime's security forces during the uprising; in fact, the corpses had been pulled from the morgue to serve as props. A French forensic scientist claimed that the Ceaușescu executions had been staged

Opposite Harun Farocki and Andrei Ujică. *Videograms of a Revolution.* 1992. 16mm film transferred to standard-definition video (color, sound), 106 min. The Museum of Modern Art, New York. Given anonymously in honor of Anna Marie Shapiro

1 Francis Fukuyama, "The End of History?," *National Interest*, no. 16 (Summer 1989): 3.
2 Mentions of media technologies are scarce in "The End of History?": "easy access to VCRs" and the fact that "color television sets [are] now omnipresent throughout China" are mentioned merely as evidence of "the abundance of a free market economy" and the growing ubiquity of consumer culture, respectively. Fukuyama, "End of History?," 8, 3.
3 Serge Daney, "Roumanie année zéro," in *La maison cinéma et le monde*, vol. 3, *Les années libé, 1986–1991* (Paris: P.O.L., 2012), 314. Unless noted, translations are my own.
4 Serge Daney, "Éloge têtu d'information," in *Devant la recrudescence des vols de sacs à main: Cinéma, télévision, information* (Lyon: Aléas Éditeur, 1992), 171.

for the camera and the real killings performed earlier, out of sight.[5] Arguments raged over the correct number of casualties. Long before "fake news" and "alternative facts" became everyday refrains, fissures appeared in the Romanian media event, giving the lie to the notion that the immediacy of television could be a guarantee of authenticity. The searing sight of death—singular, obscene, *real*—faded into fakery.

In 1992 Jean Baudrillard diagnosed it all as "Timișoara syndrome," a situation marked by "a deflation of historical consciousness."[6] The theorist who would soon infamously declare that "the Gulf War did not take place" saw in the mediated revolution a corrosion of reality and truth.[7] To him it was no anomaly but rather the apotheosis of the spurious illusion that broadcast news always already embodies. "Television," he asserted, "inculcates indifference, distance, scepticism and unconditional apathy. Through the world's becoming-image, it anaesthetizes the imagination, provokes a sickened abreaction, together with a surge of adrenalin which induces total disillusionment."[8] This argument was not without precedent: in 1927 Siegfried Kracauer had proposed an inverse relationship between the quantity of photographs in circulation and the possibility of historical knowledge, describing the mass of images appearing in the new illustrated magazines as a destructive assault on memory, a decontextualizing "flood" or "blizzard" that leveled all difference.[9] These positions lay bare the deeply vexed relationship between history and the lens-based image. The latter's claim to referentiality—that is, to testimony—sits uncomfortably alongside the capacity to make those traces mobile, to uproot them with ecstatic ease and disperse them far and wide. When images of the world are transported and recombined, some meanings are shed and others gained. A sense of derealization can take hold as concreteness and specificity wash away in the flood.

For Baudrillard, Timișoara syndrome had the virtue of making at least one thing clear: forever after, all would know that images were not to be trusted. The end of history and the end of belief in the image went hand in hand. "Never again shall we be able to look at a television picture in good faith, and this is the finest collective demystification we have ever known," he claimed. "Where better than on television can one learn to question every picture, every word, every commentary?"[10]

II

In fact, there is something more suited to this task than television—and that is an encounter with artworks that repurpose televisual coverage of historical events. Found-footage practices are often conceptualized through the Situationist concept of détournement, whereby images from the mass media are hijacked and reused in ways that subvert their original meanings, producing a critique of dominant representations. In Dara Birnbaum's *Technology/Transformation: Wonder Woman* (1978–79), for instance, the gender stereotypes of the superhero show are subject to feminist analysis, as narrative continuity is broken and looped repetition is used to incite estrangement on the part of the viewer. When artists work with videotaped news footage, as Birnbaum does in her five-channel installation *Tiananmen Square: Break-In Transmission* (1990), a different relation to the image is at stake (fig. 1). The tension between referentiality and circulation is of utmost concern. Although defamiliarization remains in play, it is less a matter of assailing petrified clichés and contesting the monoculture of television than it is a question of orienting oneself in relation to images of the world and the world of images, of grappling with the fact that history is no

5   See "Ceaușescu Execution Video Faked, Experts Say," *Associated Press*, April 30, 1990.
6   Jean Baudrillard, "The Timișoara Massacre," in *The Illusion of the End*, trans. Chris Turner (Cambridge, UK: Polity, 1994), 58; first published as *L'illusion de la fin, ou La grève des événements* (Paris: Éditions Galilée, 1992).
7   Baudrillard, "La Guerre du Golfe n'a pas eu lieu," *Libération*, March 29, 1991; reprinted in the collection *The Gulf War Did Not Take Place*, trans. Paul Patton (Bloomington: Indiana University Press, 1995).
8   Baudrillard, "Timișoara Massacre," 61.
9   Siegfried Kracauer, "Photography," in *The Mass Ornament: Weimar Essays*, trans. and ed. Thomas Y. Levin (Cambridge, MA: Harvard University Press, 1995), 58.
10   Baudrillard, "Timișoara Massacre," 60, 61.

longer something outside of representation, to be betrayed or honored, but something that takes shape in and through acts of mediation.

In *Tiananmen Square*, Birnbaum confronts the possibilities and failures of broadcasting by multiplying screens and snatching fragments from the ephemeral nowness of television, transforming them into artifacts to be encountered in new ways. Made using footage from the student-led pro-democracy protests that took place in Beijing between April and June 1989, the installation comprises four tiny LCD screens, each mounted on an armature attached to the ceiling and each playing a looped two-to-six-minute clip: a music video made in Taiwan as a gesture of solidarity with protesters on the mainland, evocatively titled "Wound of History"; images of the protests as seen on US news programs, slowed to a crawl; announcements of the end of satellite broadcasting, ordered by the Chinese state; and scenes of the alternative methods, such as fax and teletype, used to disseminate information (figs. 2–4). A fifth channel, a cathode-ray-tube monitor, plays images sampled at random from the LCD screens through a surveillance switcher, combining them into a disjunctive stream. The installation establishes a space of transmission: images once cloaked in the urgency of presentness reappear out of the past, never ceasing to migrate across sites of reception, now from LCD to CRT. As they travel, they are reshaped and remade. Birnbaum assembles a multisource, extraterritorial archive of a major event in Chinese history, the memory and discussion of which remain forcefully suppressed by the state today. Rather than allowing these materials to congeal into

Figs. 3, 4 Dara Birnbaum. *Tiananmen Square: Break-In Transmission.* 1990

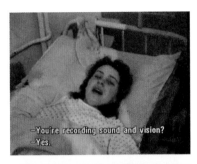

Figs. 5–7 Harun Farocki and Andrei Ujică. *Videograms of a Revolution.* 1992

a single perspective—or a lone iconic image, such as that of the unidentified man who stood in front of a column of tanks on June 5, 1989—the installation does not let them rest, keeping them forever in motion.

On one hand, *Tiananmen Square* hyperbolically stages a condition of information overload, fragmented attention, and spatial collapse, exacerbating the relationship to temporality and understanding already at play in US coverage of the protests, as in TV news more broadly. On the other hand, the installation works counter to the logic of television. In a 1991 interview, Birnbaum said, "TV tried to let you think that you could be inside, engulfed by the image and the action and the activity. But what aspect of it? Most Americans had little idea about what all this activity meant."[11] Against the medium's fantasy of clear and immediate transmission, Birnbaum foregrounds disruption and noise. Images are smeared and slowed. The LCD screens are small and cannot be viewed from an oblique angle, necessitating a close approach that solicits viewers' bodily movement and coaxes them into individual concentration on a single clip. Exploding the flow of images across multiple channels and tampering with the modes of address upon which TV news depends, *Tiananmen Square* shatters any sense that one could grasp the totality. Its gesture resonates not just in opposition to the representational economy of television but also in relation to the political context of the installation: against state control over the possibilities of expression, it affirms the impossibility of containing dissent by pointing to and participating in the stubborn afterlives of images caught live.

The problem of making meaning out of a barrage of images is central to another work exploring the relationship between the electronic image, history, and popular resistance in 1989, a work that, like Birnbaum's, pivots on a moment when a repressive state cut a live broadcast feed: Harun Farocki and Andrei Ujică's *Videograms of a Revolution* (1992), a 106-minute film assembled from footage shot by more than one hundred video cameras during the Romanian Revolution. The filmmakers steer clear of any judgment concerning the status of the dead bodies or whether the executions were staged, foregoing retrospective evaluation to instead inhabit the time of the events as they unfold. Nevertheless, everywhere throughout *Videograms* are reminders of the constructedness of representation, from the film's opening—in which a woman suffering in a hospital bed confirms that the camera is recording before testifying to the violence of the Ceaușescu regime and pleading for actions against it to continue (fig. 5)—to a point later on, when Prime Minister Constantin Dăscălescu's announcement of the government's resignation is shown from three different camera angles and then repeated because the TV station wasn't ready to broadcast the first time around (fig. 6). A British journalist reporting from the conflict delivers his speech again and again in an effort to get it right. Cameras rephotograph images displayed on screens, gleaning information secondhand (fig. 7). Farocki and Ujică anatomize Ceaușescu's final public speech, parsing the commotion in voice-over commentary, underlining how television figures as a site of manipulation and struggle. Far from creating a simple opposition between the charade of the regime and the authenticity of images produced by the people, *Videograms* asserts that every image, no matter its provenance or purpose, demands a critical reading.

What is a "videogram"? Most obviously, the neologism invokes the practice of writing and the telegram's ability to carry information across distance. We are in a space of transmission once more, a space again marked by disruption, failure, and the clash of perspectives. As Eva Kernbauer notes, "While every typewriter in Communist Romania

11 Dara Birnbaum, interview by Susan Canning, *Art Papers* (November–December 1991): 57.

had to be registered, the proliferation of video cameras was uncontrolled," opening an unregulated realm of communicative potential.[12] Meanwhile, when the videogram is understood in relation to its photo-chemical cousin, the photogram—the individual film frame—the word also gestures to an admitted partiality, a quality suggested, too, in the title's use of the plural.[13] This is a film in which disparate fragments collide, a film that knows that the plasticity of montage does not necessarily draw the image away from testimony but can, in the words of Georges Didi-Huberman, "transform the partially remembered time of the visible into a reminiscent construction, a visual form of haunting, a musicality of knowledge."[14] Faced with the multiplication of viewpoints and the superabundance of footage, Farocki and Ujică refused to throw their hands up in exasperation and deem all images disposable because the mass media made them so. The existence of all these remnants of the past may threaten the liquidation of history, but it is also a political opening, harboring as it does a polyvocality capable of challenging hegemonic narratives. Farocki and Ujică have invented a pedagogy of extraction and sequencing, creating contingent constellations of intelligibility. They embrace the role Dork Zabunyan has called the "orchestrator": the one who "accompanies the indefinite flow of these images through the ordeal of their saturation at high speeds, and assembles them in order to take the time to understand the histories that, in spite of everything, these images can pass on."[15]

Television creates its own constellations, haphazardly and often with limited fidelity to the events it relays. It abides by an illogic of collision that prefigures the experience of the internet. Dead bodies appear sandwiched between advertisements for laundry detergent and frozen foods, or right after a cheery segment about the coming weekend's sunny weather. Some acts of montage are performed with care; others are not. That which should arrest our gaze can be flattened into undifferentiation. Daney closes a text about the Romanian broadcasts with an urgent question: "How can distance be reinvented?"[16] Birnbaum's and Farocki and Ujică's interventions are two examples, however different, of how this might be done. They douse the fire of liveness, consigning televisual presence to the past and thus opening an interval of reflection. We see the already seen again, and now attend as much to the conditions of visibility as to the raw matter of distant conflict.

I I I

Baudrillard enjoins his readers to question television's "every picture, every word, every commentary." *Tiananmen Square: Break-In Transmission* and *Videograms of a Revolution* proceed down this path, but there is a bend in the road. Rather than leading to a postmodern skepticism—to the notion that the relationship between sign and referent has been definitively severed, to the idea that the image is a simulacrum devoid of any connection to the real—these artworks do indeed bring about a questioning of *every* commentary, Baudrillard's included. They never lose sight of the fact that the images they repurpose make testimonial claims that should not be ignored. Contrary to the state's attempts to pull the feed, they recirculate traces of actuality.

The woman who inaugurates *Videograms* with a direct-to-camera address from the hospital, naming the regime's violence and demanding freedom, finds her double at the film's end. After a long list of credits has attributed each shot of the film to its maker, a coda begins. A man stands within a small group of people, recounting the jealousy, hatred,

12 Eva Kernbauer, "Establishing Belief: Harun Farocki and Andrei Ujică, *Videograms of a Revolution*," *Grey Room* 41 (Fall 2010): 79.
13 While the term *photogram* often refers to cameraless photographs, such as those produced by Man Ray, it can also be used to refer to the individual frame on the filmstrip. See, for instance, Raymond Bellour, "The Film Stilled," trans. Alison Rowe and Elisabeth Lyon, *Camera Obscura* 8, no. 3 (1990): 99–123.
14 Georges Didi-Huberman, *Images in Spite of All: Four Photographs from Auschwitz*, trans. Shane B. Lillis (Chicago: University of Chicago Press, 2008), 138.
15 Dork Zabunyan, *The Insistence of Struggle: Images, Uprisings, Counter-Revolutions*, trans. Stefan Tarnowski (Barcelona: IF Publications, 2019), 70. Translation modified by the author.
16 Serge Daney, "Nicolae et Elena lèguent leurs corps à la télé," in *Devant la recrudescence*, 171.

We had no fun in life.

01:40:46:10

Figs. 8–10 Harun Farocki and Andrei Ujică. *Videograms of a Revolution.* 1992

17 Indeed, Ujică has noted the continuity between film and video: "It is only with the advent of the video camera, and the increased possibilities for lengthy and mobile recording it offers, that the process of the filmification of history can be completed." Andrei Ujică, interview by Rob White, *Film Quarterly* 64, no. 3 (Spring 2011): 68.
18 Ujică, interview by White, 68.
19 Taking refuge in the question mark in the title of the 1989 essay, Fukuyama has pointed to developments as diverse as nationalist populism, Islamic fundamentalism, and the "identity politics practiced on university campuses" as sharing a demand for dignity that continues to fuel the motor of conflict long after the end of the Cold War. Francis Fukuyama, *Identity: The Demand for Dignity and the Politics of Resentment* (New York: FSG, 2018), preface.

and suffering of the Ceaușescu years (fig. 8). As he recalls the many who died, he is overcome with emotion and exhorts those listening—whether gathered around him or around their televisions—to "never forget to support each other, because that's what life demands of us." He wishes them a happy Christmas and signs off with "Long live free Romania." It would be a betrayal of ethical responsibility to encounter such testimonies and dismiss them as emptied of history, to debunk them as mere mystifications undeserving of our good faith. The face of the other can reach us through the airwaves. The monologues that bookend *Videograms* serve as warnings against cynicism; they are sentries watching over all the images that pass between them, many of which assert the power of video as a historical witness and agent. How hardened must a gaze be to look upon Chinese students putting their bodies on the line and see only media spectacle, only a constructed picture? Standing alone in front of Birnbaum's diminutive viewing stations, one might pause and consider what traces of the real persist within and through the unreality of the screen, and how best to meet their address. If these artworks guide their viewer towards a critical questioning of the production and circulation of images, they equally suggest that seeing at a distance can yield a crucial recognition: we all inhabit the same world, a world held in common.

On Christmas Day, 1989, the streets of Bucharest were deserted. The voice-over in *Videograms* tells us that everyone was glued to their television screens, waiting for the communiqué that would announce the outcome of the Ceaușescus' hasty trial (figs. 9, 10). In this anticipatory silence, Farocki and Ujică offer a rare moment of metacommentary in voice-over, striking at the heart of their undertaking: "Since its invention, film has seemed destined to make history visible. It has been able to portray the past and to stage the present. . . . Film was possible because there was history. Almost imperceptibly, like moving forward on a Möbius strip, the side was flipped. We look on and have to think, if film is possible, then history, too, is possible." "Film" is used loosely here, within a work integrally dependent on the durational capacity, lightweight apparatus, and speed of transmission proper to video.[17] Photochemistry may be increasingly obsolete, but film—in the generic sense of a time-based medium able to capture and circulate traces of reality—is more possible than ever. Farocki and Ujică assign to the moving image the tremendous burden of not just registering but producing our relation to the past. There will inevitably be times when the medium will buckle under the load, but the task is to search for ways to bear it.

In a 2011 interview, Ujică commented on this passage of the voice-over, deeming it "an ironic reference to the posthistoricist theses from the beginning of the 1990s, when it was being rumored that we have reached 'the end of history.'"[18] Such theses have not aged well; even Fukuyama has admitted that "history" is alive and well.[19] The anxiety provoked by its mediated transmission, meanwhile, has only intensified in the age of fiber optics. Watching the flow of events, we have more reason than ever to mistrust what we see. State police still fire on protesters, revolutions still go bad, and images are still made to lie. Yet casting a glance back to 1989, to the age of camcorders and broadcasting, and to some of the artistic responses it provoked, offers a reminder that our crisis has come before: each new medium recycles old fears. Rather than become caught in a polemical threnody about the collapse of reality or turn numb to the ethical demands that reach us through images, we might better ask Daney's question once more: How can distance be reinvented? Perhaps one of the things moving-image artworks can teach us is how to find a clearing, however slight, as the storm blows in.

CHANNEL ZERO
Aria Dean

During the 2018 trial of Chicago police officer Jason Van Dyke for the murder of Laquan McDonald, Van Dyke's lawyers presented as part of their defense a 3D-animated reconstruction of the event. The animation "included overhead views of the scene and what McDonald would have looked like from Van Dyke's point of view" based on the officer's account of the event, Chicago's WGN9 reported. In this narrative, "McDonald moved toward Van Dyke—a direct contradiction to state testimony that said the teen walked away from police."[1] Beyond state testimony, the officer's statement and the animation's visual account directly oppose recovered and widely circulated dashcam footage of the event.

Much of Van Dyke's trial was spent discussing the validity of the animation when compared with the footage, eyewitness accounts, and state testimony. The prosecution argued that not only was the animation absurd—in it, McDonald moves toward Van Dyke at an inhuman speed, covering roughly twenty-five feet in the span of four seconds—but its other basic details differed from what was shown in the recovered clip: McDonald's dress, the quality of light at the time of the shooting, and so on.

Details aside, the very suggestion that a simulation made from a subjective verbal account could be weighed against video evidence in a court of law signals a reconfiguration in the life of the recorded image, a paradigmatic shift in our allegiance to the evidentiary truth of the moving image. What's more, instances like the McDonald case display this yet-unnamed new paradigm's mobilization on a mass scale, in sinister real-world applications beyond the annals of media theory. A court's willingness to accept the animation as evidence and debate it in detail is surprising. This apparent glitch—or potential new feature—in our system of thought prompts an assessment of the impact of the police brutality video in contemporary culture and its status as a kind of widely distributed vernacular cinema. Since at least 1992, when video of Rodney King being beaten by the LAPD and the acquittal of the offending officers sparked riots, it has been clear that such evidence does little to ensure legal justice in instances of police brutality against Black people. For the past three decades, public opinion has tended toward a progressive outrage in such instances, but verdicts do not reflect this sentiment.

This consistent divergence, a cognitive dissonance between representation and reality when it comes to anti-Black violence—and, frankly, a confusion about which is which—has only become more dramatic. As Louis-Georges Schwartz wrote in 2016, another landmark year in America's negotiations with its rampant and violent anti-Blackness, "an examination of recent examples suggests that the problem is not just one of representation but also one of interpretation."[2] The important question is no longer how such material can be used to prevent police violence. It is, rather, why *doesn't* it? What does it do instead, and how?

In "Counter-forensics and Photography," Thomas Keenan writes that "photographic evidence must be considered in terms of the forum or the debate into which its testimony is entered."[3] In the case of the

Opposite Black Audio Film Collective and John Akomfrah. *Handsworth Songs*. 1986. 16mm film transferred to high-definition video (color, sound), 58:33 min. Courtesy Smoking Dogs Films and Lisson Gallery

1 Julie Unruh and Nancy Loo, "Jurors Watch 3D Animation of Laquan McDonald Shooting," WGN9, September 25, 2018, wgntv. com/news/jason-van-dyke-trial-continues-tuesday/.
2 Louis-Georges Schwartz, "In Plain View: Video Evidence," *Artforum* 54, no. 10 (Summer 2016).
3 Thomas Keenan, "Counter-forensics and Photography," *Grey Room* 55 (Spring 2014): 65.

police brutality video, this forum is not just a court of law but also the spectacular public tribunal of the online sphere. In both arenas, such videos should be figured as "operational images," to borrow Harun Farocki's term. Operational images are those that "do not portray a process but are themselves part of a process."[4] The police brutality clip is embedded in at least two processes. On one hand, it is mobilized as a part of the judicial process. On the other hand, it is mobilized in the social process of grappling with anti-Blackness. Both of these processes participate in the production of social reality, and they repeatedly tangle with one another.

American Artist's *2015* explores this entanglement, fixing as its object a narrative point just before the police brutality event and its resulting documentation. Created for the 2019 exhibition *My Blue Window*, mounted at the Queens Museum, the work is an immersive high-definition video depicting an early morning in New York in 2015 (fig. 1). The calm atmosphere becomes eerie when we realize that we are looking at the dashcam footage from a police car (figs. 2–4). The windshield is overlaid with a computer interface: a kind of digital dashboard for predictive policing, an artificial-intelligence tool that forecasts the locations of possible crimes before any crimes occur. As the patrol car drives through Brownsville, our view is layered with navigation-system graphics noting the purported likelihood of burglaries, even murder. Occasionally, scrolling text declares "CRIME DETERRED"—even though there is nothing happening and no one on the streets. Within this hallucinatory, video game–like world, viewers are both implicated in and made keenly aware of multiple perspectives, placed on the dividing line between Blue Lives and Black Lives. We begin to see the ways in which historical bias may be encoded within seemingly neutral technologies and how an area or an entire population may be deemed criminal in the absence of actual crime. The artwork presents a moment of overlap between two points of view: that of a specific technical computer/camera, trained to search and destroy, and its human agent, the police officer.

Through this combination, *2015* raises questions about perspective and viewer identification in moving images, drawing on decades of film-theoretical discourse arguing that the "ideological effects of perspective depend upon identification with the camera."[5] According to psychoanalytic film theory and popular film discourses, a first-person point of view produces empathy and identification from the audience. American Artist has stated that, when viewing the video, "you're in the position of the police officer, watching dashcam footage. It has this voyeuristic aspect to it. The title 'My Blue Window' is alluding to the mental space of the police officer, identifying with this notion of blueness. How does that make you feel? It doesn't make me feel good."[6]

And yet we cannot forget the presence of the computer/camera in *2015*. The predictive-policing algorithm and its visual representation will likely appear quite nonsensical to the viewer, producing not identification but alienation. The video displays an operationalized image produced for computers, not for humans—or, at the very least, an image made in tandem with and subject to computer logic. The computer latches onto elements of the visual field that would seem, to the human eye, utterly unrelated to criminal activity, laying bare the absurdities of the pattern-recognition tools upon which entire industries rely. Absurdity turns to horror when we consider that the use of these tools has often been a matter of life and death. "A computer can of course process images," Farocki writes, "but it needs no real images to determine the veracity or the falsity of the image it is fed."[7] The computer looks for patterns endemic to its own logic and does not care if reality has another story to tell.

Fig. 1 Installation view, *American Artist: My Blue Window*, Queens Museum, New York, 2019

Figs. 2–4 American Artist. *2015*. 2019. High-definition video (color, sound), 21:56 min. The Museum of Modern Art, New York. Fund for the Twenty-First Century

4 Harun Farocki, notes for *Eye/Machine III* (2003) on the artist's website, harunfarocki.de/installations/2000s/2003/eye-machine-iii.html.
5 Kaja Silverman, "The Gaze," in *The Threshold of the Visible World* (London: Routledge, 1996), 125. Silverman is referring, in turn, to Jean-Louis Baudry's foundational essay "Ideological Effects of the Basic Cinematographic Apparatus," *Film Quarterly* 28, no. 2 (Winter 1974–75): 39–47.
6 American Artist, "Slowing Down to See Black and Blue," interview by Julie Hoangmy Ho, *New York Times*, October 23, 2019.
7 Harun Farocki, "War Always Finds a Way," in Farocki and Rodney Graham, *HF, RG: Harun Farocki, Rodney Graham*, exh. cat. (Paris: Black Jack/Jeu de Paume, 2009), 110.

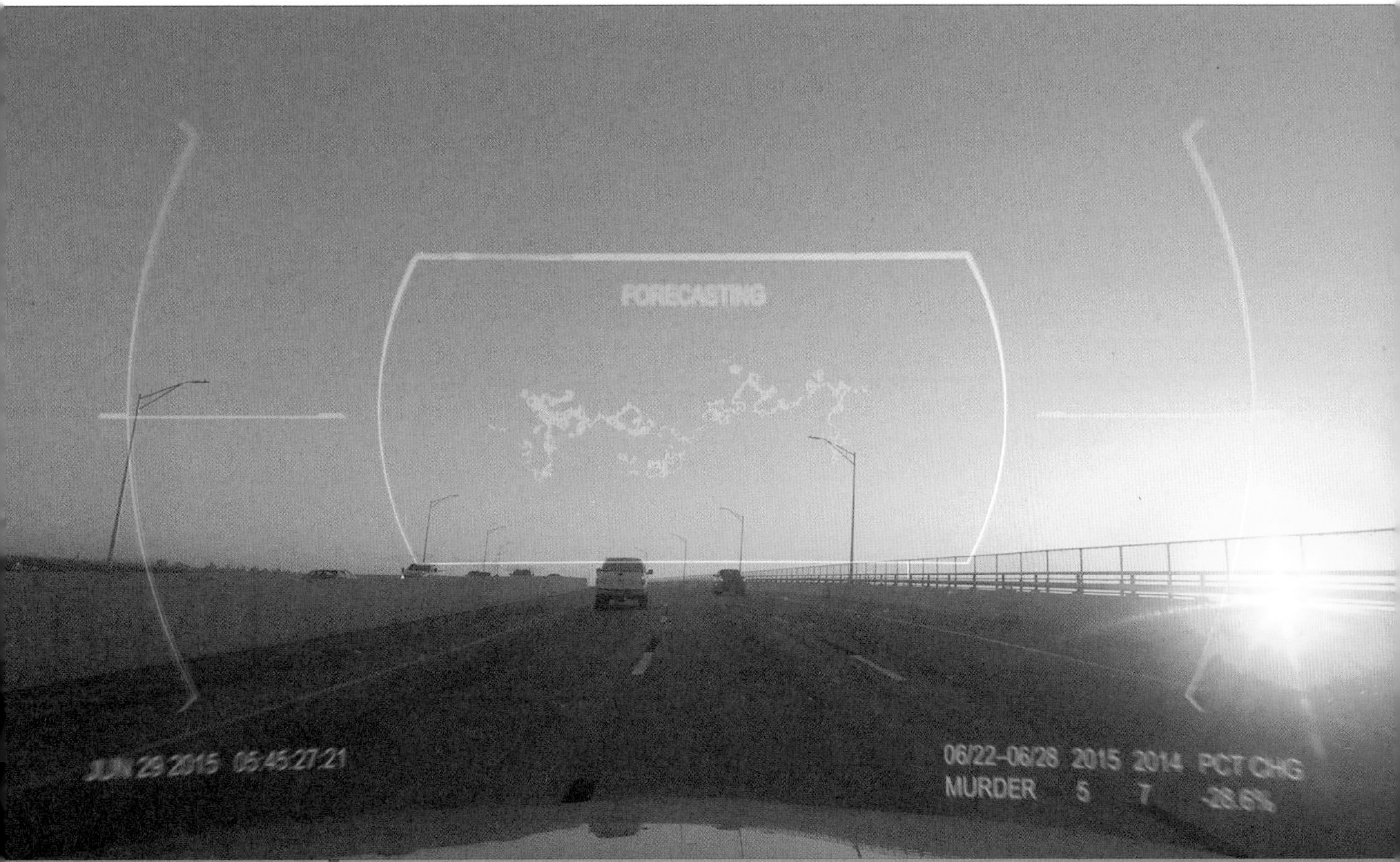
FORECASTING
JUN 29 2015 05:45:27:21
06/22–06/28 2015 2014 PCT CHG
MURDER 5 7 -28.6%

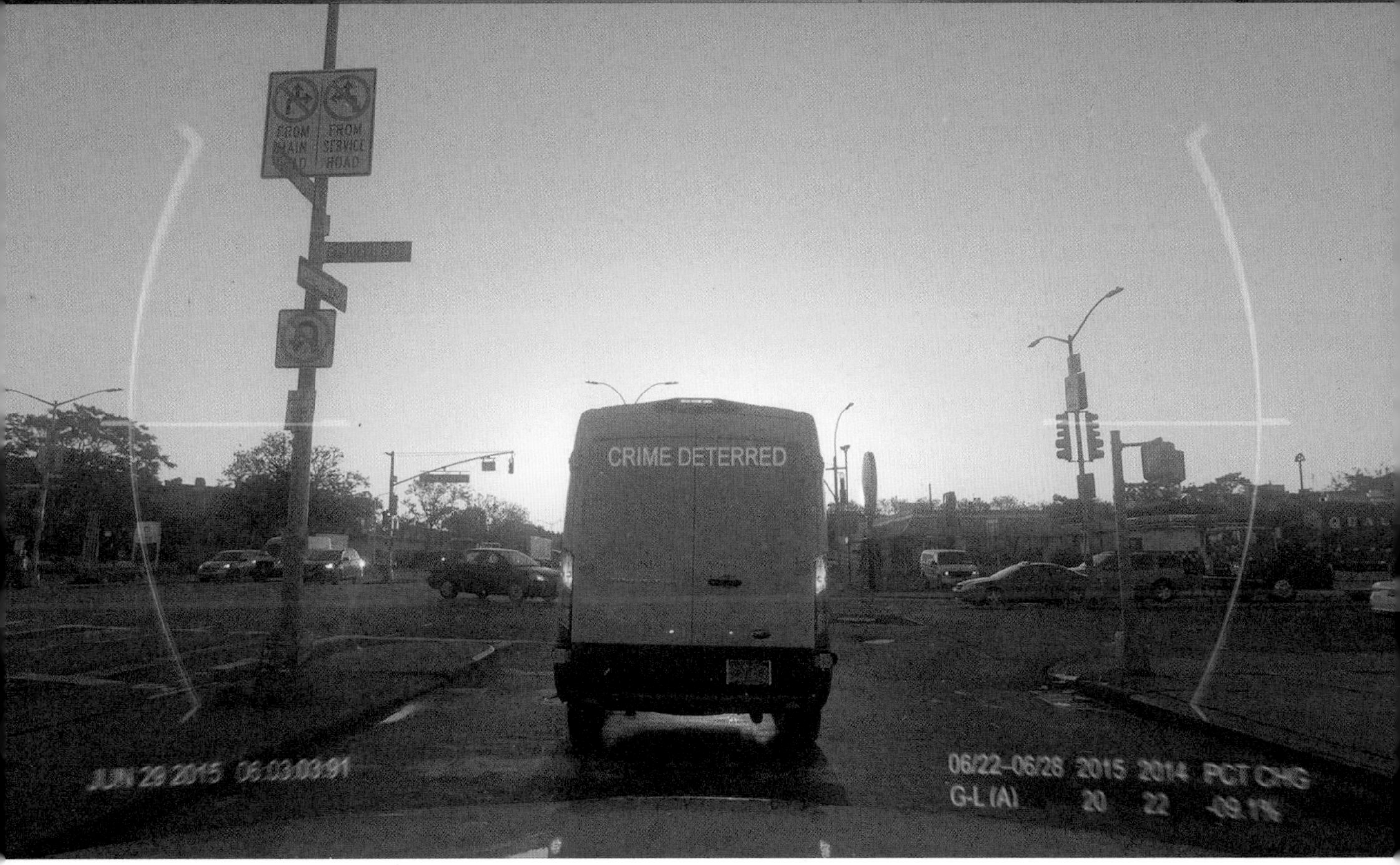
FROM SERVICE ROAD
CRIME DETERRED
JUN 29 2015 06:03:03:91
06/22–06/28 2015 2014 PCT CHG
G-L (A) 20 22 -09.1%

Fig. 5 Peter Friedl. *Liberty City*. 2007. Standard-definition video (color, sound), 1:11 min. MACBA Collection. MACBA Foundation. Fundación Repsol Collection

Farocki continues, "If a program in a sequence of images only draws in what it is looking for, whether it be colored lines as markers in an aerial landscape or the baseboard in the hall of a research institute used to orient an autonomous robot, then we're seeing a kind of disavowal of what is being marked."[8] Here Farocki parallels Sylvia Wynter's 1992 text "No Humans Involved," in which the philosopher describes the ways in which the official language applied to Black males in policing in Los Angeles in the 1990s absented them as subjects. For Wynter, this operation is an ideological one that finds its expression through language as a "classifying logic," with the phrase "No Humans Involved" placing the "Black Conceptual Other outside 'the universe of obligation.'"[9] American Artist presents an updated, immediately technical manifestation of this absenting, a double bind: literally and figuratively, no humans are involved—yet crime is spotted everywhere. *2015* displays a disturbing and dominant regime of vision that not only excludes Black men from "the universe of obligation" but also produces a technical program of the functional and conceptual annihilation of the Black subject.

This collusion of computer/camera and police officer in the "eye" through which we witness the scene in *2015* models the imbrication of technology and ideology we experience in human action. In much of their recent work, American Artist is preoccupied with the notion of "Blue Life," a concept that plays on the color of police uniforms across municipalities and converts it into a lifestyle or a kind of identity. The emergence of Blue Lives Matter as a countermovement to Black Lives

8 Farocki, "War Always Finds a Way," 110.
9 Sylvia Wynter, "'No Humans Involved': An Open Letter to My Colleagues" (1992), *Forum N.H.I.: Knowledge for the Twenty-First Century* 1, no. 1 (Fall 1994): 44, 57.

Matter is curious, since *police* is, to the understanding of most, a verb or a job. To identify as police—unlike identifying as, say, an accountant—is to identify as a fleshy gear in the machine of state-sanctioned violence (justified by the rhetoric of liberal peacekeeping), while at the same time asking for such a life to matter within the same largely humanistic conceptual edifice in which we must ask for Black lives to matter.[10]

In the age of Blue Lives Matter, to view a scene from the perspective of a police officer is to view it from a peculiar—yet fully explicated—form of parasubjectivity. Such parasubjectivity is not unique in our age, as it coincides with other mutations of the subject brought on by our total imbrication, materially and conceptually, in the operations of speculative capitalism, in our entanglement with digital networks, and in a new awareness of our bodily unsovereignty gained courtesy of COVID-19. At all levels, we are a machine for living, killing, and dying. The police, specifically, are, as Steve Martinot and Jared Sexton write, "a machine for killing and incarcerating."[11] Through an appropriation of the *blank*-lives-matter formula, Blue Lives Matter marks but one expression of a near-totalizing binding together of life, identity, the state, and—in the twenty-first century—the machine. At the same time, as they do this killing and incarcerating, the police are intended to appear neutral; to follow Nico Baumbach's framing, their business can only be carried out effectively if we—and they—normalize it.[12] It is for this reason that the transition of Blue Life to a viable concept is so intriguing. Through it, the police become a paradox—a spectacular and identitarian neutrality.

The question of neutrality, and of perspective, is thus even more crucial to the police brutality video than is immediately obvious. Consider, for instance, the murder of Philando Castile by a police officer in Minnesota in 2016. The primary record of the event is citizen-produced video content in the form of the live stream of the incident made by Castile's partner, Diamond Reynolds, who was sitting in the passenger seat next to him. Normally, such first-person footage would elicit identification with Reynolds because of its formal mechanisms (if not because of her and Castile's glaring innocence): Reynolds and the camera coincided, and the video was circulated in real time (the live stream theoretically indicating a rawness, a lack of tampering). The mere existence of critical public discourse about the clip—for example, about Reynolds's and Castile's personal histories, an exercise repeated with each instance of police brutality—is disturbing evidence not only of the strange difficulty of identifying with the Black subject but also of the inability of classical film and media theory to describe the functions of such an object.

Surely, part of the difficulty in exploring the structural dynamics of the police brutality video is the ethical urgency of its contents. However, approaching it and the so-called cinema of policing overall formally and structurally is an equally rich political-theoretical project, to which *2015* and other artworks have contributed. For instance, Peter Friedl's *Liberty City* (2007) attempts to deconstruct the "standard historical scene" of the anti-Black police brutality event by "inverting [its] dramatic structure."[13] To do this, Friedl stages an altercation between Black men and a white police officer in which, instead of the officer assaulting the Black men, the Black men beat the officer (fig. 5). The scene is shot from across the street, at night, on grainy digital video, recalling the Rodney King tape and the general aesthetic of vernacular video. But can a police brutality clip, whether staged or real, have a dramatic structure? According to Frank B. Wilderson III, probably not. The narrative arc of a slave who is Black, he writes, is "not an arc at all, but a flat line."[14]

10 Fred Moten and Denise Ferreira da Silva, among other artists and academics, have offered an alternative anti-humanistic reading of the phrase "Black lives matter," but in the popular imagination it generally remains within the realm of humanist understandings of proper life and living.
11 Steve Martinot and Jared Sexton, "The Avant-Garde of White Supremacy," *Social Identities* 9, no. 2 (2003): 176.
12 Nico Baumbach, *Cinema/Politics/Philosophy* (New York: Columbia University Press, 2018), 44–47.
13 Erna Hecey Gallery, notes for Peter Friedl's *Liberty City* (2007), ernahecey.com/artists/27-peter-friedl/works/9384-peter-friedl-liberty-city-2007/.
14 Frank B. Wilderson III, *Afropessimism* (New York: Liveright, 2020), 102.

NO.

NOTHING

O

NO

NOTHING

Figs. 6, 7 Tony Cokes. *Black Celebration*. 1988. Standard-definition video (black and white, sound), 17:11 min. The Museum of Modern Art, New York. Friends of Education and Committee on Media and Performance Funds

Liberty City isolates and models the same principle that actual videos of police brutality exhibit time and time again: that something sort of wrong happens when such an altercation is represented to us. Even inverted, it is unsatisfying—there is no triumph. At best (or worst), the video has you waiting for another cop to show up and for the violence to capsize. This flatness is strange and difficult to describe. It's like the old optical illusion: "Is it two faces or a vase? Faces? Or vase?" It's both.

Friedl and the vernacular objects he was at once replicating and prefiguring enact Denise Ferreira da Silva's claim that "blackness . . . functions as a nullification of the whole signifying order that sustains value in both its economic and ethical scenes."[15] In da Silva's calculation, when blackness (-1) figures into any equation where the other term is life (1), the result is zero. And so Blackness in general cannot make an appeal to ethics, to retributive justice, because it is figured as a form of nonlife: no humans are involved. If this is so, then Blackness certainly cannot make a successful ethical appeal in the context of video or cinema—where the signifying order is a cornerstone for producing meaning. If semiotics cannot *do* Blackness, then film/video, so grounded in this humanistic interpretive exegesis, sputters as it encounters the police brutality clip and cannot make it do meaningful work in the service of evidence, or justice, or expression. Structurally focused works such as *2015* and *Liberty City* begin to uncover the way in which "power in postmodern society works as a process of production, rather than as a drama of representation."[16]

Further, when Black Life and Blue Life come into conflict, a conceptual fissure opens. Here two parasubjective forms (already paradoxes in themselves) clash: nonlife disguised as life (the police), and life disguised as nonlife (the Black subject). This event is a voided scene, at once both spectacular and neutralized. Viewing the police brutality video as a voided scene changes the terms of engagement. It is not just an image of power producing itself through anti-Black violence; it is a key part of the process of such power producing itself. Where American Artist pursues the collusion between technology and ideology in the clip's prefatory, foreboding moment, Friedl isolates the violent event in time and, disposing of its technical-judicial operationality, provides an inroad to the event's affective social life. Friedl's video and others are thus brief snapshots of the larger structural situation of anti-Blackness. The terms of life and nonlife amount to zero within the frame's bounds. The police brutality clip presents the police procedure as pure form, a set of nothing. This is made possible by the fact that, as Calvin Warren writes, "pure form is the consequence of perfect death, black death."[17]

In any scenario, such videos cannot generate force on their own. They must enter into a technical-affective complex of processes that we know better as "the justice system" or more broadly as "politics." Time and time again, they generate action and affect in both the judicial and the social registers, and it is at this point in the larger operation, just after the capture of the event of brutality and its entrance into circulation, that the two registers become thoroughly entangled. This larger process, obviously, is a cycle. We've seen it many times over. It begins with surveillance, sparks with the police brutality clip, ignites into a riot, and loops.

There's always a point in the cycle where someone says that riots are bad because they don't have a goal, and then someone else has to argue that this is in fact the point. In the 1960s, Guy Debord wrote of the 1965 Watts riots in Los Angeles, "What is irrational is to appeal legally against a blatant illegality."[18] Tony Cokes's video *Black Celebration* (1988) references Debord's text on Watts in its first frame and then repeatedly throughout (figs. 6, 7). Interspersing Debord's

15 Denise Ferreira da Silva, "1 (life) ÷ 0 (blackness) = ∞ − ∞ or ∞ / ∞: On Matter beyond the Equation of Value," *e-flux journal*, no. 79 (February 2017).
16 Steven Shaviro, "Film Theory and Visual Fascination," in *The Cinematic Body* (Minneapolis: University of Minnesota Press, 1993), 22.
17 Calvin Warren, "The Catastrophe: Black Feminist Poethics, (Anti)form, and Mathematical Nihilism," *Qui Parle* 28, no. 2 (December 2019): 357.
18 Guy Debord, "The Decline and Fall of the Spectacle-Commodity Economy" (1965), trans. Ken Knabb, in *Situationism: A Compendium*, ed. Debord et al. (Bread and Circuses, 2014), n.p.

writing with other commentary and a montage of newsreel footage of the Watts uprising and uprisings in other Black neighborhoods in the 1960s, Cokes's work gives shape, if not meaning and narrative, to the 1965 general revolt and events like it. Viewed on a longer historical arc, however, *Black Celebration* investigates the inherent limitations of Debord's idea that the uprising can somehow exceed or militate against its consumption as public image or spectacle. Such a view of the relationship between Black Americans, uprisings, and spectacle has been outpaced by the technological and political reality of the United States. The argument can no longer be made that Watts (or any of the many other uprisings of the last hundred years) might figure as a total "revolt against the spectacle . . . against dehumanized life" and result in a "fulfillment of true human and social nature and transcend the spectacle."[19] The notion that the riot can directly create such a rupture is a twentieth-century dream.

Instead of transcending the spectacle, the past seventy years have seen the increasing recuperation of radical action: the riot, the revolt, and the uprising have been yoked into the larger police procedural operation and regime of representation that deftly maintain a white-supremacist status quo. The uprising is no longer only a "rebellion against the commodity," as Debord termed it; it is an image absorbed into an operational system. The structure of *Black Celebration* puts a fine point on this. Cokes strings together newsreel footage from 1960s uprisings in Los Angeles, Boston, Newark, and Detroit, and they ultimately blur into an indistinct montage within which Los Angeles does not feel that different from Newark, nor Boston from Detroit. He treats these events as generic, and together they form a typology. For the contemporary viewer, the 1960s do not feel that different from the 2020s. From the vantage of 2022, *Black Celebration* appears to be a meditation on the doomed repetition of such images across decades—on the fact that, as Wilderson said in 2020, "the police stations may be burning and the anarchists might be fighting the pigs in hand to hand combat, but civil society itself is actually being strengthened through these pitched battles."[20]

The uprisings in *Black Celebration* seem to haunt John Akomfrah's *Handsworth Songs* (1986). The film, produced by the Black Audio Film Collective, cobbles together newsreel footage, still images, on-the-ground interviews, and B-roll from the 1985 Handsworth riots in Birmingham, England (fig. 8). It is a video essay without a singular author, instead relying on first-person accounts and documentary moving images to tell its story, if there is one to be told. At one point in the film, a woman frankly tells a local journalist, "There are no stories in the riots, only the ghosts of other stories." Her comment, though brief, frames the whole project. Much like *Black Celebration*, *Handsworth Songs* emphasizes the fact that the event has been and will be repeated. Both works make us painfully aware that the riot may once have been a real action, in which the physical gesture of rebellion was inseparable from actual rebellion. Now, kickstarted by the police brutality event, it might primarily be a part of a morbid, libidinal "economy of the loss of meaning, a hyper-economy," as Martinot and Sexton write. "It is this hyper-economy that appears in its excess as banal; a hyper-injustice that is reduced and dissolved in the quotidian as an aura, while it is refracted in the images of the spectacular economy itself."[21]

This being said, while *Handsworth Songs* might not tell a story, it does ask us to settle in the gap between story and meaning, an awkward place of chaotic and unmanageable raw significance. In this sense, with its nonlinear, collaged sensibility, *Handsworth Songs* has an effect

19 Debord, "Decline and Fall," n.p.
20 Frank B. Wilderson III, interview by Aria Dean, *November* 0, interview no. 2 (2020), novembermag.com/content/frank-b-wilderson-iii.
21 Martinot and Sexton, "Avant-Garde of White Supremacy," 177.

similar to today's media, with its haphazard arrival on our doorsteps. Online, a deluge of images and videos circulate without a narrator, offering themselves up for interpretation by human and machine audiences alike. They are not the ghosts of something else; they are a kind of dumb matter, the muck of Western life. And the key element of their condition is that they do not mean anything. On the grounds of representation, they cannot be evaluated for what they show. These objects both imply and suffer from an interpretive problem—which is to say not that they are divisive but that they illustrate the very problem of interpretation itself, and therefore the very problem of subjectivity. They appear at first glance to provide case studies for a political impasse, for a repeated failure of empathy for Black human beings and a larger failure of the political system to recognize this ongoing failure. But beyond this, they detail the very complicated problem of politics, subjectivity, and the production of meaning. The fight for justice has been a fight for consensus, rooted in an understanding of politics based on a paradox: the unified subject. As Baumbach argues, following Rancière, "Subjectivization . . . posits an impossible unity."

If politics is "the contestation over the meaning of appearance," as Baumbach writes, then the police brutality clip and its before and after—surveillance and uprising, respectively—cannot be approached at the level of the political.[22] It is clear that in the public sphere no consensus will be reached over the *meaning* of the appearance of state violence and its aftermath; the content may continue to galvanize the willing, but otherwise it merely retraces a schism. And anyway, structurally and theoretically, the scenario might be void, modeling an empty equation where nonlife confronts nonlife, making a death with no narrative

Fig. 8 Black Audio Film Collective and John Akomfrah. *Handsworth Songs*. 1986

22 Baumbach, *Cinema/Politics/ Philosophy*, 47.

drama. But counterintuitively, perhaps in being emptied, being a set of nothing, the clip may be a non-narrative object around which narrative can and does produce itself—in the multitude of objects made and circulated by a variety of actors, a multiplicity of stories whose very problem is that none of them are ghosts.

This is probably where I would have left things were I writing this early in 2020, as I was meant to do; I was, at the time, wholly pessimistic about the police brutality clip's operations. However, after that summer's uprisings, the machinations of this loop are less clear. Something definitely happened, and it was definitely somehow because of videos of police brutality and, at the same time, videos of protest. Yet that something was not the transcendence of spectacle, nor was it the abolition of the police. It certainly did not mark the end of anti-Blackness.

In another essay, in another few years, with a little more distance, I'll probably have the clarity to make an argument about the fact that much of the war that summer was waged on the battlefield of video— that along with seizing property and narrative, people seized the moving image. They were familiar enough with its operations, in the sense that I have tried to outline above, to manipulate its structure and circulation for the benefit of those who needed it most. For better or for worse, the next time around, power will have to find a few new protocols.

Stan VanDerBeek
(American, 1927–1984)

MOVIE-DROME. 1964–65
Dome theater with 3 16mm films (black and white and color, sound; varying durations), 320 black-and-white and color 35mm slides, 3 16mm slide projectors, and sound, dimensions variable

In November 1965, Stan VanDerBeek wrote to the Rockefeller Foundation requesting support for *Movie-Drome*. VanDerBeek was constructing a prototype of this "experience machine," as he called it, at the Gate Hill Artists' Cooperative in Stony Point, New York, in a prefabricated aluminum grain-silo dome. There he had begun testing both the technical equipment and experimental film and slide materials that were to be projected across the dome's thirty-one-foot-diameter interior surface as a way to facilitate a certain "mental mutation" in its audience, lying prone on the floor. As VanDerBeek would frequently reiterate, most famously in his 1965 manifesto "Culture: Intercom and Expanded Cinema," the Gate Hill *Movie-Drome* was conceived as one node in a worldwide network served by an "artist interchange." VanDerBeek explained in his letter to the Rockefeller Foundation that he sought to develop an "'international picture language' that overcomes verbal and semantic blocks" as a means to "relieve world tensions." "The most important concept of this 'experience machine,'" he wrote, "is to make the world audience 'self' conscious of itself, which I think is an essential step in the bringing about of peaceful co-existence." To this end, he proposed that *Movie-Drome* would present programs of varied audiovisual content ranging in length from thirty minutes to two hours, including what he called "the entire visual history of western man . . . from the Egyptians to the present." Employing 16mm film projectors, slide projectors, overhead projectors, spotlights, and a quadraphonic sound system, *Movie-Drome* brought together newsreels, found film, and VanDerBeek's own animated and collage-based films, along with drawings and art historical, anthropological, commercial, and popular images, to create a disjunctive, overlapping, and ever-transforming field of information.

At the height of Cold War tensions, deploying such a media-technical apparatus in service of world peace might have seemed an urgent task for artists, technological advances having long fueled idealistic visions, originating in the Global North, of worldwide communication systems as means for overcoming enmity (despite so much evidence to the contrary). VanDerBeek's vision for "international education" had an avowed target: *Movie-Drome*, the artist announced—mobilizing the linguistic tropes of international aid—would allow "the over-developing technology of part of the world to help the under-developed emotional-sociology of all of the world to catch up to the 20th century." As he saw it, *Movie-Drome*'s media, operating with an accelerated "visual velocity" and a distinctly teleological disposition, might be deployed as both an expansion of the public sphere and a tool of subjective modernization worldwide—part of a global development apparatus. It is not surprising that this vision appealed to the Rockefeller Foundation, a key player in forging new scripts of global governance; the organization gave the artist a grant in 1965.

Most accounts of *Movie-Drome* recall that it debuted as part of the New York Film Festival, when, on September 18, 1966, Shirley Clarke, Annette Michelson, Agnès Varda, Paul Morrissey, Andy Warhol, and other figures from New York's downtown scene were bused to Gate Hill for VanDerBeek's expanded-cinema program *Feedback*. VanDerBeek did not see his "culture intercom" realized beyond the Stony Point prototype, except for one staging in a temporary geodesic dome for a Central Park "Design-in" in 1967. What might have happened if the artist's test subjects had hailed not from New York's artistic avant-garde but from the imaginary world community he envisioned? What if his apparatus of subjective transformation had been grafted onto the so-called developing world, armed, as it was, with a spirit of idealism that paid little attention to its own ambiguous and ambivalent political disposition? The Egypt in VanDerBeek's "visual history of western man" was not that of the 1960s—a country then marked by the violent legacies of colonial rule and by modernization engineered by economic-development experts from the North. And *Movie-Drome*'s art-historical images, like the institutions and discourses then advancing Western culture, were far from neutral; they came with a political disposition, too. This is not to suggest that the intended targets of *Movie-Drome*'s expanded network in Africa, Asia, and Latin America would have been any less cognizant of the powers at play in such a setup or any less likely to interrupt, appropriate, critique, allegorize, or expose the political and economic entanglements at work. It is, rather, to wonder how the work's discordant and heterogeneous aesthetic potentials might have functioned *otherwise* within an expanded geography, how they might have been uncoupled from normative and technocratic regimes bent on particular modes of modernization and even become tools of solidarity. In an era when the near-instantaneous global circulation of audiovisual media takes place not through "culture intercoms" but through smartphones and personal computers, an era that has witnessed the rise of peer-to-peer sharing and citizen journalism along with artistic engagements with these platforms, such questions are particularly salient. At a world scale, how might VanDerBeek's project have navigated or repurposed such ambivalences? How might it have operated differently, even helping to shift its *own* disposition as a burgeoning media-technical apparatus with a developmental telos, complete with regulatory function? How could it have put its heterogeneity to work to test the new types of political space that might open up within an ever-transforming public sphere?

FELICITY D. SCOTT

Top Interior of *Movie-Drome*, Stony Point, New York, 1964, with VanDerBeek at right

Bottom Exterior of *Movie-Drome*, Stony Point, New York, 1964

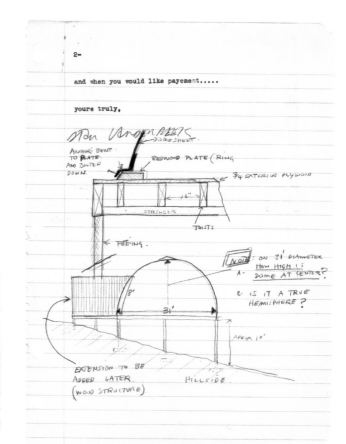

S.VanDerBeek
Gate Hill Rd.
Stony Point N.Y.
Sept 25,64

Dear Mr Fanckboner:

Thanks for your letter of Sept 23,....

1- I have decided to simplify the problem of the opening
   in the dome to expidite the whole thing...the order
   will be for a complete 3I foot diameter aluminized steel
   dome,the opening I will cut into after the dome has been
   put up...

2- I assume that this will be as easy to do if not easier
   in making the opening come out to the size I want,unless
   you think It would be better to do it before in your
   fabrication stage..????(I plan to cut the opening with
   an acetylene torch..)

CONVENTIONAL SLIDE UP DOOR.

CUT OUT AFTER DOME IS UP WITH TORCH......AND
REENFORCE WITH ANGLE IRON..... 12' OPENING. 8' MSA APP

3- The dome will have the conventional sliding door you
   offer ﬂﬂﬂ as standard equiptment on the dome...is this
   sliding door any larger than it would be on the smaller
   domes..?? how wide and high is this sliding door..???

4- I am putting up my footings now and plan to built a wood
   deck   feet square,frankly I have no clear plan for
   fastening the dome to this deck,and if you have any
   suggestions I am open to them....(see sketch on other
   sheet...)

5- In sumary: please proceed at once with my order for the
   3I foot diameter aluminized steel dome,I won't have any
   changes made in your fabrication,the dome should have
   the standard sliding door, and fiberglass cap,the water-
   -proofing sealing strips,etc...please include the standard
   anchor clamp fastened to the sheets...note: are the anchor

   clamps bolted to the sheets or rivited..???prefer bolted.

   please send me complete billing and instructions,also how

2-

and when you would like payement.....

yours truly,

Stan VanDerBeek

DOME SHEET.
ANCHOR BENT TO PLATE. AND BOLTED DOWN.
REDWOOD PLATE (RING
3/4 EXTERIOR PLYWOOD
STRINGER
JOISTS
FOOTING.
NOTE:
A- ON 3I' DIAMETER HOW HIGH IS DOME AT CENTER?
B- IS IT A TRUE HEMISPHERE?
8'
3I'
APPROX 10'
EXTENSION TO BE ADDED LATER. (WOOD STRUCTURE)
HILLSIDE

Top Letter from VanDerBeek to manufacturer of *Movie-Drome*'s dome,
September 25, 1964

Bottom *Movie-Drome* under construction, Stony Point, New York, 1964

44

Top   VanDerBeek in *Movie-Drome* at Design-In, Central Park, New York, 1967
Bottom   The artist leads a tour of *Movie-Drome* for the New York Film Festival, Stony Point, New York, September 1966

45

Marta Minujín
(Argentine, born 1943)

SIMULTANEIDAD EN SIMULTANEIDAD. 1966
Documents, slides, and ephemera, dimensions variable

Simultaneidad en simultaneidad (*Simultaneity in Simultaneity*) was a sprawling, ambitious event that promoted a new understanding of the ways in which media could transform self-representation and enable simultaneous global communication. Though physically centered in the auditorium of the now-legendary Instituto Torcuato Di Tella in Buenos Aires, the work was part of a much larger project for which Minujín proposed to create a triangular connection, via telephone and satellite, to Happenings staged concurrently in New York and Berlin by artists Allan Kaprow and Wolf Vostell, respectively.

Minujín created the work in the context of her own series of 1960s Happenings, events akin to technological laboratories in which the artist subjected audiences to a barrage of stimuli. In *Simultaneidad en simultaneidad*, a select group of local celebrities and intellectuals gathered at the Institute, where they were captured in video and audio recordings and then invited to see and hear the results. Crucially, Minujín included closed-circuit television systems, which let participants see themselves "crowned" by the frame of the TV.

Media, especially television, were central to Latin America's modernization during the 1960s. Minujín's intention to reveal the "setting power of media," as she put it, emerged from her participation in a series of Buenos Aires–based discussions led by cultural critic Oscar Masotta and engaging sociologists and artists such as Roberto Jacoby, Eduardo Costa, Raúl Escari, and David Lamelas. The group came to believe that the cultural conditions of the time rendered the implicit immediacy of Happenings outdated; instead, they conceived of a new—and more critical—"art of media."

For Masotta, this "art of media" might become a revolutionary art. He wrote, "Works of mass communications media are susceptible . . . to receiving political content; I mean from the left, truly convulsive, capable really of merging a 'revolutionary praxis' with an 'aesthetic praxis.'" For such artists, legitimately critical art had to reveal the increasing centrality of media by emphasizing the circulation of information itself; and so, paradoxically, by embracing the immateriality they sought to denounce, they conflated art with public relations. Minujín, however, went even further. She intended to create a hyperbolic version of the new culture of technological mediation and narcissism propelled by TV's proliferation. *Simultaneidad en simultaneidad*, one of her most important media works from the 1960s, pointed toward the audience as an image bouncing back onto itself. It also reenvisioned the figure of the artist herself, who commanded the Happening wearing a golden jumpsuit: an embodiment of a fully artificial public persona, capable of bringing the future into the present.

INÉS KATZENSTEIN

Simultaneidad en simultaneidad, Instituto Torcuato
Di Tella, Buenos Aires, 1966

Simultaneidad en simultaneidad, Instituto Torcuato
Di Tella, Buenos Aires, 1966

Raindance Corporation
(USA, founded 1969)

PROTO MEDIA PRIMER. 1970
Standard-definition video
(black and white, sound), 16:05 min.

MEDIA PRIMER (SHAMBERG). 1971
Standard-definition video
(black and white, sound), 16:29 min.

What is a "media primer"? Between 1970 and 1971, Raindance Corporation, the media collective founded in 1969 by Frank Gillette, Paul Ryan, Michael Shamberg, Ira Schneider, and others, produced no less than three of these videos-cum-tutorials. In the context of political activism and countercultural insurgency increasingly aimed at corporate broadcasting networks and government media, the term *primer* might have several meanings. While it could indicate an elementary textbook in alternative uses of media technology, it could just as well be a more metaphorical reference to explosive materials, since a "primer" is also a compound that ignites an explosive when exposed to an electrical impulse. None of the videotapes reveal any explicit sense of purpose, producing instead a vague sense of being "in" and "with" electronic media. Raindance had already established such an impulse in *The Rays* (1970)— a twenty-three-minute-long tape that features diagonal distortion patterns created by interference from the broadcast TV signals of a nearby transmitter. Behind this layer of signal disturbances, Raindance members and friends are seen hanging out on a California beach, passing the camera carelessly from hand to hand like the joints they have obviously been smoking, commenting flippantly on signal interferences and whatever else ties them together in this heady moment of communal taping. A random-seeming segment, it only makes sense in terms of the relationships it establishes between cameras, hands, bodies, the sun, the beach, and electromagnetic events. Willfully neglecting all tenets of normal TV formatting, the work adopts atmosphere, not narrative, as its key mode. A short excerpt from *The Rays* reappears in one of the Media Primers, as if to underscore the general significance of this strategy.

The budding community-video scene of the early 1970s quickly encountered problems of presentation and attention: their public gatherings were captured in hours of footage, but people rarely had time to watch the unedited tapes. This was the underground version of the continuity of TV time, the never-ending live feed subtending broadcast programming's array of precisely delimited slots and formats. Reconstructing yet also deformatting this feed, the Media Primers, consisting of a jumble of uncommented footage, challenge attentive viewing by zapping from one disjointed situation to the next. As in so much early video art, the works' images seem to come in swarms: having low iconicity and weak contextual framing, they appear to exist in and of themselves rather than for viewers. Separately, many situations recorded in the Media Primers were related to underground media politics of the time—there are sequences with radical icons like Abbie Hoffman and conversations with ordinary media users, and scenes sourced from political campaigns, surveillance systems in public places, and kids trying out video equipment. Yet the Media Primers offer no advice on what to do with this material; random-seeming breaks, silences, and technical disturbances only serve to underscore this lack. Whether as textbooks or explosives, the early works of Raindance seem to operate on a single principle, promoting, for better or worse, the reality of electronic media as a new existential vector.

INA BLOM

Top Still from *Media Primer (Shamberg)*
Bottom Still from *Proto Media Primer*

Top and bottom Stills from *Media Primer (Shamberg)*

Top Still from *Media Primer (Shamberg)*

Bottom Still from *Proto Media Primer*

53

TVTV
(USA, active 1972–1979)

FOUR MORE YEARS. 1972
Standard-definition video
(black and white, sound), 61:28 min.

The arrival in 1967 of the first truly portable video camera, Sony's Portapak, inspired a new generation of artists and journalists to create what they dubbed "guerrilla television": alternative news reports shot in a quick-and-dirty style on black-and-white half-inch reel-to-reel tape, unencumbered by the standards and protocols of network television. By 1972, individuals from three of the most active collectives—Videofreex, Raindance Corporation, and Ant Farm—came together to form Top Value Television, or TVTV, with the aim of covering the US presidential election conventions of that year. *Four More Years*, their peek into the Republican National Convention in Miami Beach, Florida, which would heartily endorse the reelection of Richard Nixon, quickly became a classic documentary, breaking through to mainstream audiences when it was ultimately broadcast on TV stations around the country. "Whatever Porta-Paks do that TV doesn't is what we want to do," the group stated in a 1972 issue of *Radical Software*, the primary journal of the movement. "This means injecting ourselves into the material, intimate access to situations, the use of special lenses."

Despite its countercultural origins and nontraditional aesthetic, TVTV's tape seems by today's standards to be carefully evenhanded in its coverage. Avoiding voice-over narration or, indeed, any overt editorializing, the crew compiled cinema-vérité-style footage and off-the-cuff interviews with convention staffers, politicians, attendees, protesters, and major network journalists to give viewers a behind-the-scenes look at how a major media event is produced. Profiling young Nixon supporters, for instance, TVTV allows them to respond to claims in the news that their actions were staged by higher-ups. "We're here because we want to be here, not because it's just for publicity," one young woman states emphatically to the camera. "We really believe in Nixon, and that's why we're here!" Another Nixonite stresses that they "weren't paid to be here." Cutting back and forth between a pro-Nixon squad cheering inside the convention center and fatigues-clad "Vietnam Veterans Against the War" protesting outside, the tape asks viewers to reach their own conclusions. Delving deep into the makings of a monumental "pseudo-event" composed for major network cameras, *Four More Years* leveraged the novelty of alternative media to gain a level of access unthinkable in the tightly controlled political spectacles of later decades.

ED HALTER

Opposite Ant Farm's Doug Michels (left) carries a Sony Portapak at the 1972 Republican National Convention, from the TVTV booklet *Prime Time Survey*, 1974

Top and bottom Stills from *Four More Years*

55

Top Still from *Four More Years*

Bottom Members of TVTV, Miami Beach, c. 1972. Left to right, standing: Michael Couzins, Michael Shamberg, Allen Rucker, T. L. Morey, Maureen Orth, Skip Blumberg, and Chip Lord. Seated: Frank Cavestani, Jody Sibert (holding picture of Richard Nixon), Megan Williams, Anda Korsts, Tom Weinberg, Steve Christiansen, Wendy Appel, Hudson Marquez, and Martha Miller. In pool: Nancy Cain

Fujiko Nakaya
(Japanese, born 1933)

FRIENDS OF MINAMATA VICTIMS—VIDEO DIARY. 1972
Standard-definition video
(black and white, sound), 20 min.

Fujiko Nakaya, best known for her fog sculptures—expansive, shape-shifting clouds of natural water that she has created since the 1970s—played a central role in the development of media art in Japan. As a member of the collective Experiments in Art and Technology, she coordinated various projects for its Pepsi Pavilion at Expo '70 in Osaka and organized the Tokyo site of the exhibition *Utopia Q&A 1981*, which let participants in far-flung cities pose questions to each other via Telex. From 1972 to its dissolution around 1975, Nakaya was also a key member of the Tokyo-based video-art collective Video Hiroba, which promoted and experimented with video as an alternative to hegemonic mass-media networks. In 1974 she published a Japanese translation of the 1971 book *Guerrilla Television*, by Michael Shamberg and Raindance Corporation, which described how handheld video cameras might be a tool in resisting the concentrated power of broadcast television. And from 1980 to 1992 she ran Tokyo's Video Gallery SCAN, which created a vital link between local and international video scenes.

Nakaya created *Friends of Minamata Victims—Video Diary* for *Video Communication: Do-It-Yourself Kit* (1972), the first Japanese exhibition devoted exclusively to the medium and the unofficial founding event of Video Hiroba. The work records the eighty-first day of protests outside the Tokyo headquarters of the Chisso Corporation, whose chemical plant had released toxic waste in Minamata Bay, leaving thousands with mercury poisoning. Unlike contemporaneous documentary films and photo-essays that chronicled the difficulties faced by victims primarily by examining the rural pollution site near Minamata, Nakaya's work reveals the stories of victims as presented by the protesters in Tokyo. After documenting their morning exercises, their confrontations with Chisso's guards, and their attempts to engage passersby, Nakaya showed them the footage on a portable television. Taking advantage of her video camera's playback function to create a feedback loop, the artist gave protesters the chance to see themselves represented sympathetically and intimately within the television's frame, while also turning the video camera into a tool for communication between different shifts of protesters.

As Nakaya saw it, the dynamic situation she created on-site, facilitated by video technology, was itself the artwork; the remaining footage is merely a document of that event. Accordingly, she has specified that the video document should be shown on a portable television monitor similar to the one she used in front of Chisso's headquarters in 1972.

NINA HORISAKI-CHRISTENS

MINAMATA PATIENTS ARE THE
VICTIMS OF MERCURY POISONING
WHICH CAN BE TRACED TO EATING
THE FISH AND SHELLFISH CAUGHT
IN MINAMATA BAY POLLUTED BY
CHISSO COMPANY'S INDUSTRIAL
DRAINAGE.

Richard Serra
(American, born 1938)
Carlota Fay Schoolman
(American, born 1949)

TELEVISION DELIVERS
PEOPLE. 1973
Standard-definition video
(color, sound), 6 min.

In 1973, Richard Serra acquired his first batch of video equipment; soon after, he and Carlota Fay Schoolman made *Television Delivers People*. A scrolling text with yellow letters on a blue background, the video is accompanied by a Muzak soundtrack whose insipid strains suggest a commercial motivation. At first glance, *Television Delivers People* might recall a public service announcement or a cheaply produced advertisement. The text itself, however, works against such assumptions. A string of implacable aphorisms announces the video's oppositional stance. "The product of television, commercial television, is the audience," one line reads. "Television delivers people to an advertiser. . . . You are the product of television."

Indeed, *Television Delivers People* is an incisive rebuttal to the utopian claims made for video in that era, addressing the stark hierarchy between television and the fledgling medium. Television, as Serra put it in a 1979 interview, "had a stranglehold" on those wanting to make videos, for the systems and protocols that enabled video's transmission on TV were subject to structures of control and predicated fundamentally "on the capitalistic status quo." The textual content of *Television Delivers People* was drawn from the proceedings of a New York conference on the topic of mass media: Serra excised quotes from various articles to make the script. Schoolman and Serra then obtained a character generator from New York's public television station, Channel 13, to produce the work, which made its first on-air appearance as a sign-off to a program on a local station in Amarillo, Texas, followed by a showing on WTTW in Chicago.

Television Delivers People's graphic presentation underscores the urgency of the artists' message: in short, that the ostensibly democratizing capacities of video by artists and citizen activists are mediated by entrenched, infrastructural considerations. In this way, the video anticipates by decades a critique of the liberatory rhetoric supporting the internet as a transparent communications medium.

PAMELA M. LEE

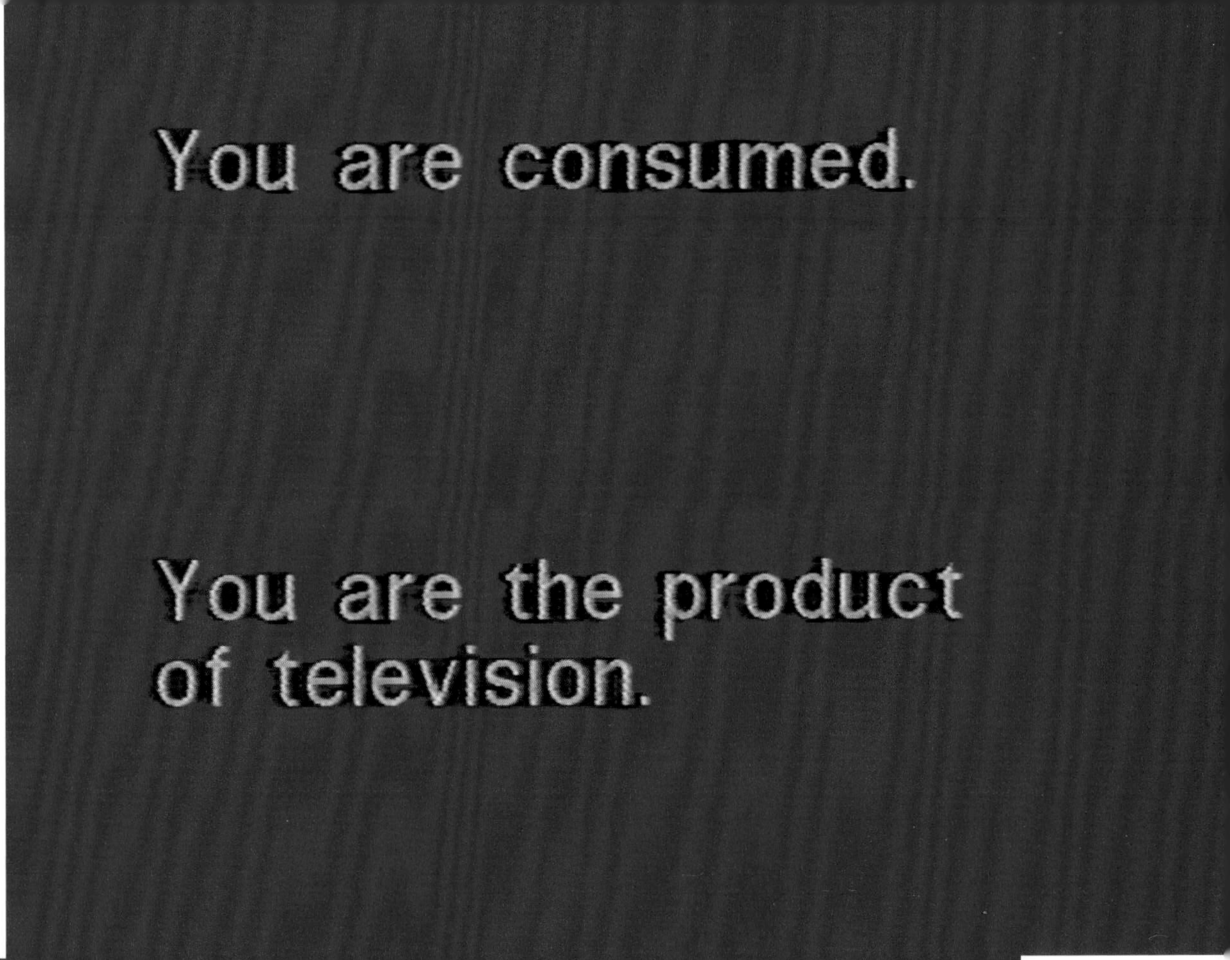

You are consumed.

You are the product
of television.

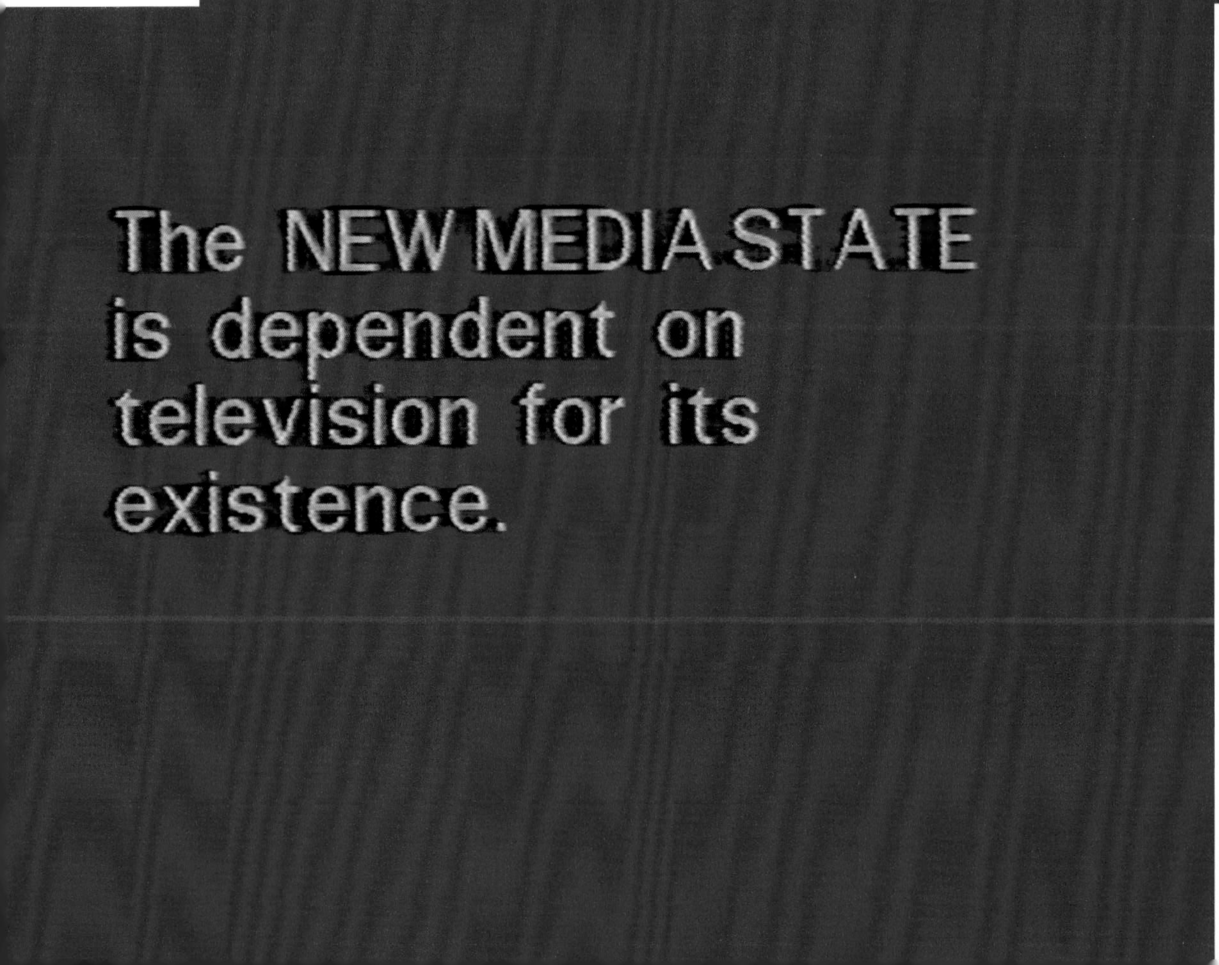

The NEW MEDIA STATE
is dependent on
television for its
existence.

Commerical television
delivers 20 million
people a minute.

In commercial broad-
casting the viewer
pays for the privilege
of having himself sold.

What television
teaches through
commercialism is
materialistic
consumption.

The NEW MEDIA STATE
is predicated on
media control.

What goes on over the news is what you know.

It is the basis by which you make judgements, by which you think.

There is a mass media compulsion to reinforce the status quo.
To reinforce the distribution of power.

General Idea
(Canada, active 1969–1994)

TEST TUBE. 1979
Standard-definition video
(color, sound), 28:15 min.

General Idea, the Canadian trio of artists AA Bronson, Felix Partz, and Jorge Zontal, created *Test Tube* as a television program. "It is the first artist video I know of that uses the color palette of television, rather than the color palette of film," Bronson said in 2010. The video's commitment to the conventions of television extends beyond color, as it mixes a variety of familiar formats—talk show, commercial, soap opera—to subversive effect. After being presented in the Canadian pavilion of the Venice Biennale in 1980, it was eventually broadcast in Switzerland, Spain, Canada, and the United States.

Test Tube's rhythms will be familiar to anyone with access to cable television. It starts as a talk show, with the artists as the hosts of a fictional space called the Color Bar Lounge. Sitting at a high table, they critique the art world and the media, occasionally turning to the camera to deliver pithy sound bites: "We think of television as our test tube. Not only to test market the Color Bar Lounge, but also to test out new formulae for making art consumable." This is followed by the main program: scenes from a soap opera–style narrative about Marianne, a painter juggling her baby, her artistic integrity, and the art market. These scenes are cut short in a familiarly frustrating way by commercials for fictional products such as Nazi Milk and Liquid Assets (the latter featuring a cameo by artist Marina

Abramović). *Test Tube* is characteristic of General Idea's "viral method," their practice of "infecting" popular forms like television, advertising, and marketing rather than rejecting them, and redeploying them toward alternative social orders. "We don't want to destroy television," Zontal stated. "We want to add to it. We want to stretch it until it starts to lose shape."

Eight years later, in 1987, with their first "AIDS" painting (an appropriation of artist Robert Indiana's iconic "LOVE" image), General Idea would refocus their efforts on HIV/AIDS activism, harnessing virality as form, metaphor, and fact of life. *Test Tube* mimics the conventions of television, satirizing its subliminal and not-so-subliminal messages. But it also points to the art world's hermeticism and to the necessity of working in the public realm, especially as popular media failed to represent the HIV/AIDS epidemic accurately, if at all.

SIMON WU

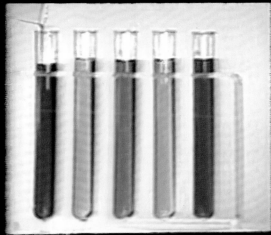

GENERAL IDEA'S
COLOR BAR
LOUNGE

CADA (Colectivo Acciones de Arte) (Chile, active 1979–1985)

¡AY SUDAMÉRICA! 1981
Standard-definition video (black and white and color, sound), 12 min.

On July 12, 1981, the Colectivo Acciones de Arte (Art Actions Collective), or CADA, arranged to have six small airplanes flown in military formation over the city of Santiago, Chile. As the aircraft crossed the sky, the five members of CADA—visual artists Lotty Rosenfeld and Juan Castillo, writer Diamela Eltit, poet Raúl Zurita, and sociologist Fernando Balcells—tossed out bundles of leaflets, releasing approximately 400,000 sheets in all. Echoing the snowcapped peaks of the Andes, which served as a dramatic backdrop, showers of paper cascaded onto the neighborhoods below. The pamphlets poetically proclaimed, "Each individual who works for the expansion of the space of his or her life . . . is an artist. . . . The work of expanding the conditions of everyday life is the only valid staging of art/the only exhibit/the only work of art that lives."

Collaborator Eugenio Téllez recorded the event from one of the planes, while more than one hundred other artists took photographs and captured video footage from points throughout Santiago. That documentation provided the material for this video, which also features scrolling excerpts from the leaflet's text. The action deliberately summoned Chileans' collective memory of the aerial bombing of the national presidential palace eight years earlier—a decisive event in the coup d'état that overthrew the democratically elected government of Salvador Allende—and obliquely encouraged Santiago's citizens to reclaim the city and remap it in ways that would counter the restrictions imposed by the new military regime. Photographs of the performance and the pamphlet text were published in the Chilean opposition publication *APSI* in August 1981, and a single-channel version of the video was screened in New York that fall at The Museum of Modern Art, in the exhibition *Video from Latin America*. Playing the liberating potential of flight against the very real threat of severe punishment by the government, *¡Ay Sudamérica!* (*Oh, South America!*) distributed CADA's lyrical missive on a wide scale.

JASON DUBS

ESPACIOS DE VIDA ES UN
ARTISTA".
LO QUE SIGNIFICA QUE DIGAMOS
EL TRABAJO EN LA VIDA COMO
UNICA FORMA CREATIVA Y QUE
DIGAMOS COMO ARTISTAS QUE
EL TRABAJO DE AMPLIACION
DE LOS NIVELES HABITUALES DE
VIDA ES EL UNICO MONTAJE DE
ARTE VALIDO/ LA UNICA OBRA

AY SUDAMERICA

CUANDO USTED CAMINA ATRAVESANDO ESTOS LUGARES Y MIRA EL CIELO Y BAJO EL LAS CUMBRES NEVADAS RE-
CONOCE EN ESTE SITIO EL ESPACIO DE NUESTRAS VIDAS: EL COLOR PIEL MORENA, ESTATURA Y LENGUA, PENSA-
MIENTO.

Y ASI DISTRIBUIMOS NUESTRA ESTADIA Y NUESTROS DIVERSOS OFICIOS: SOMOS LO QUE SOMOS; HOMBRE DE LA
CIUDAD Y DEL CAMPO, ANDINO EN LAS ALTURAS PERO SIEMPRE POBLANDO ESTOS PARAJES.
Y SIN EMBARGO DECIMOS, PROPONEMOS HOY, PENSARNOS EN OTRA PERSPECTIVA, NO SOLO COMO TECNICOS O
CIENTIFICOS, NO SOLO COMO TRABAJADORES MANUALES, NO SOLO COMO ARTISTAS DEL CUADRO O DEL MON-
TAJE, NO SOLO COMO CINEASTAS, NO SOLAMENTE COMO LABRADORES DE LA TIERRA.

POR ESO HOY PROPONEMOS PARA CADA HOMBRE UN TRABAJO EN LA FELICIDAD, QUE POR OTRA PARTE ES LA
UNICA GRAN ASPIRACION COLECTIVA/SU UNICO DESGARRO/UN TRABAJO EN LA FELICIDAD, ESO ES.
"NOSOTROS SOMOS ARTISTAS, PERO CADA HOMBRE QUE TRABAJA POR LA AMPLIACION, AUNQUE SEA MENTAL
DE SUS ESPACIOS DE VIDA ES UN ARTISTA."
LO QUE SIGNIFICA QUE DIGAMOS EL TRABAJO EN LA VIDA COMO UNICA FORMA CREATIVA Y QUE DIGAMOS, COMO
ARTISTAS, NO A LA FICCION EN LA FICCION.

DECIMOS POR LO TANTO QUE EL TRABAJO DE AMPLIACION DE LOS NIVELES HABITUALES DE LA VIDA ES EL UNI-
CO MONTAJE DE ARTE VALIDO/LA UNICA EXPOSICION/LA UNICA OBRA DE ARTE QUE VIVE.
NOSOTROS SOMOS ARTISTAS Y NOS SENTIMOS PARTICIPANDO DE LAS GRANDES ASPIRACIONES DE TODOS, PRE-
SUMIENDO HOY CON AMOR SUDAMERICANO EL DESLIZARSE DE SUS OJOS SOBRE ESTAS LINEAS.
AY SUDAMERICA.
ASI CONJUNTAMENTE CONSTRUIMOS EL INICIO DE LA OBRA: UN RECONOCIMIENTO EN NUESTRAS MENTES; BO-
RRANDO LOS OFICIOS: LA VIDA COMO UN ACTO CREATIVO...
ESE ES EL ARTE/LA OBRA/ESTE ES EL TRABAJO DE ARTE QUE NOS PROPONEMOS.

COLECTIVO ACCIONES DE ARTE
JULIO 1981   C.A.D.A.

Nam June Paik
(American, born Korea. 1932–2006)

GOOD MORNING, MR. ORWELL. 1984
Standard-definition video (color, sound), 38 min. Edited by Skip Blumberg

A triumphant response to George Orwell's bleak portrayal of television as a tool of manipulation and repression in his famous novel *1984*, Nam June Paik's legendary New Year's Day simulcast was a utopian extravaganza of televisual transmission. The work was broadcast live on public television via the Bright Star satellite from studios in New York and Paris (linked with Germany and South Korea), bringing together material from vastly different sources, including pop-music videos, avant-garde performance, experimental music, video art, and dance. "I want to show [television's] potential for interaction," Paik said, "its possibilities as a medium for peace and global understanding. It can spread out, cross international borders, provide liberating information, maybe eventually punch a hole in the Iron Curtain." Combining live and taped contributions by artists and performers Laurie Anderson, Joseph Beuys, John Cage, Merce Cunningham, Peter Gabriel, Allen Ginsberg, Philip Glass, Takehisa Kosugi, Charlotte Moorman, Oingo Boingo, John Sanborn, Sapho, and others—many of which Paik manipulated electronically as they aired—this groundbreaking spectacle upended the form and the content of mainstream television and turned a global satellite network into a conduit for cross-disciplinary and transnational collaboration.

Good Morning, Mr. Orwell reached twenty-five million viewers worldwide in its original broadcast, coproduced by New York's public-access station WNET with French National Television and the Centre Pompidou, and it lives on in various edits, including a single-channel format edited by video artist Skip Blumberg. In keeping with Paik's conception of "protons and electrons" as the raw materials of his medium, scrolling text along the bottom of Cunningham's segment reads, "FEEDBACK . . . Cunningham's image shuttling between New York and Paris at the speed of light; like an endless mirror. 92,000 miles between each image." Infused with both wonder and anxiety—the latter intensified by a series of technical glitches and delays—the work is a striking portrait of a world on the brink of total interconnectivity.

ERICA PAPERNIK-SHIMIZU

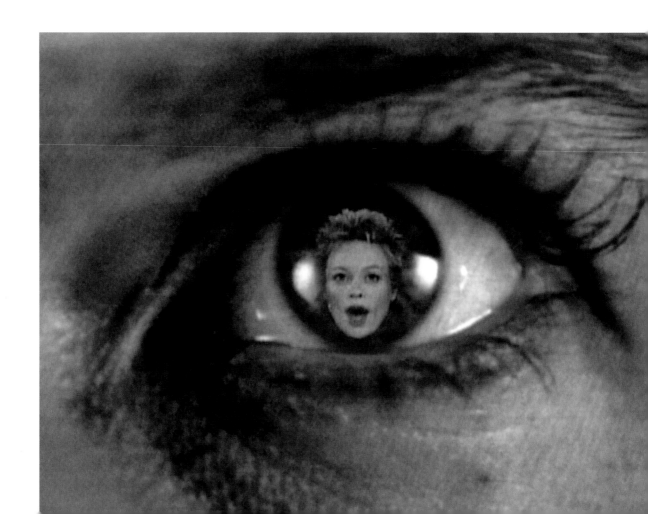

Right Music video for the 1986 song "This Is the Picture (Excellent Birds)," by Peter Gabriel, featuring Laurie Anderson

Top Live performance by Sapho of "TV Is Eating Up Your Brain" with video effects by Paik, including a superimposed image of George Orwell

Bottom Live performance by Merce Cunningham mixed with video clip of Salvador Dalí

Top Still from John Sanborn and Dean Winkler's *Act III* (1983), featuring music by Philip Glass

Bottom Live comedic interlude by Mitchell Kriegman and Leslie Fuller

Top Live performance by John Cage

Bottom Live performance by Merce Cunningham (with delayed satellite feedback) mixed with video clip of Astor Piazzolla playing the bandonion

Martha Rosler
(American, born 1943)

IF IT'S TOO BAD TO BE TRUE, IT COULD BE DISINFORMATION. 1985
Standard-definition video (color, sound), 16:26 min.

If It's Too Bad to Be True, It Could Be DISINFORMATION is both a disruption and a warning. The artist interrupts the relentless flow of information that comprises televised news, deploying video's capacity for recording and replaying broadcast TV in order to unmask seemingly neutral reportage as manipulated media. Featuring network news coverage of Cold War political and military campaigns in Latin America, the work shares its title with a 1984 *New York Times* article reporting on Soviet and American strategies to control global headlines by purposely disseminating false or speculative information.

The video begins with flashes of programming interspersed with static: a newscaster's voice fades in and out, intoning words such as "allegation," "United States," "Nicaragua," "Soviet Union," and "MiGs," while fragmented news footage of ships, talking heads, and military marches rolls through electronic snow under a transcript of the stuttering, disrupted audio. Next come previews of upcoming news segments and a commercial for the Canon A-1 camera. Then, suddenly, an interlude without any interference: footage of President Ronald Reagan defending anti-Sandinista rebels, a Nicaraguan group that US officials would soon begin funding surreptitiously—and illegally—via arms sales to Iran. (These events were part of the so-called Iran-Contra Affair, which was revealed to the American public a year after Rosler's prescient work.) After a pause, the video slowly returns to the fragmented news coverage that appeared at the outset. This time, however, the audio and transcript feature different word combinations, and only snippets of the images punctuate the static on an otherwise black screen. The work concludes with a final suite of uninterrupted scenes: reports about US war games in Puerto Rico and an American fugitive said to be supporting Cuba's activity in Latin America by helping drug smugglers. At the very end is a commercial for the US Army, a glossy fiction of war heroics set to a patriotic jingle. The continuous sequence—following the constant disruption of what has come before—is all the more jarring for its seamlessness.

Rosler's interventions denaturalize the newscast, giving the lie to its supposed neutrality and making visible the tricky relationships—and plain trickery—at the intersection of truth and falsity, transparency and secrecy, signal and noise. War simulations and Army ads blend the real and the unreal, just as news reports use previously recorded footage, file tapes, photographs, and digital maps to represent the "live" event. Even the Canon A-1 has a part to play, as the artist has long questioned the evidentiary value of the photographic image. Rosler's video punctures the continuous stream of information—and hidden ideological agendas—in the American media. The work's haltingly fractured sections, as if redacted, suggest that the ostensibly unaltered material that follows must be viewed just as critically: as news pieces that are inevitably partial.

ERICA DIBENEDETTO

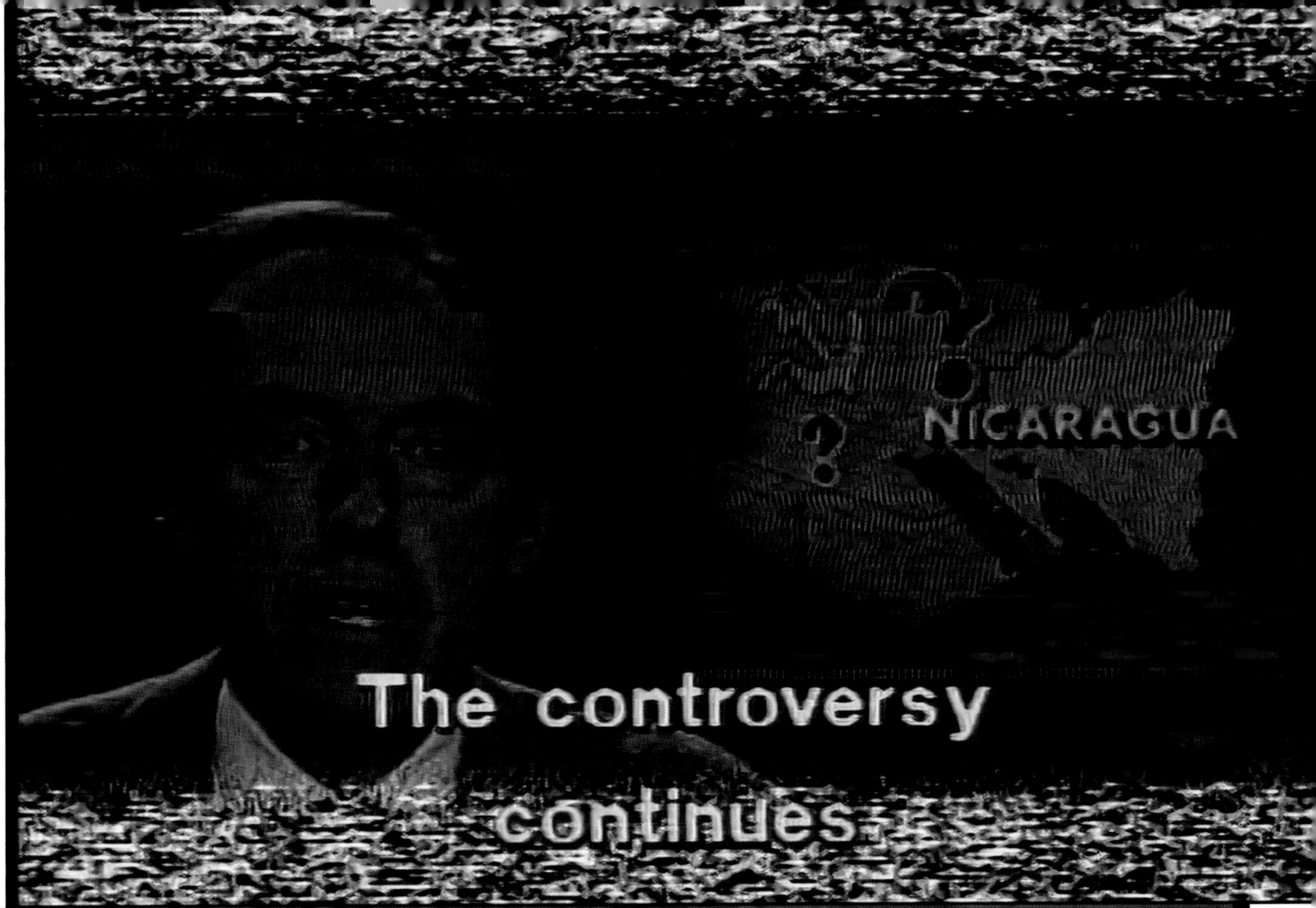

The controversy

continues.

America

might be sent

to the region

military maneuver is

seen here as

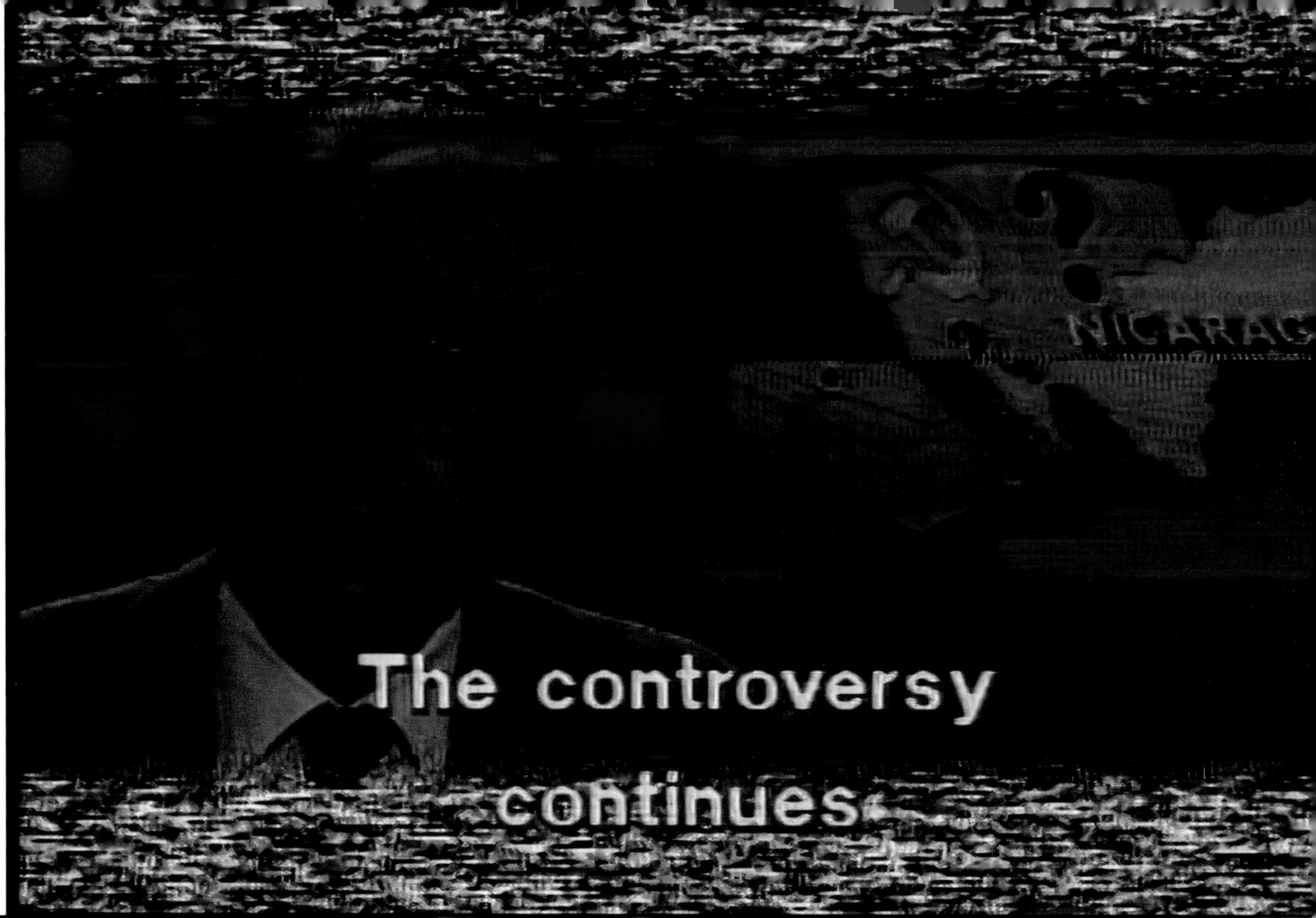
NICARAG
The controversy
continues

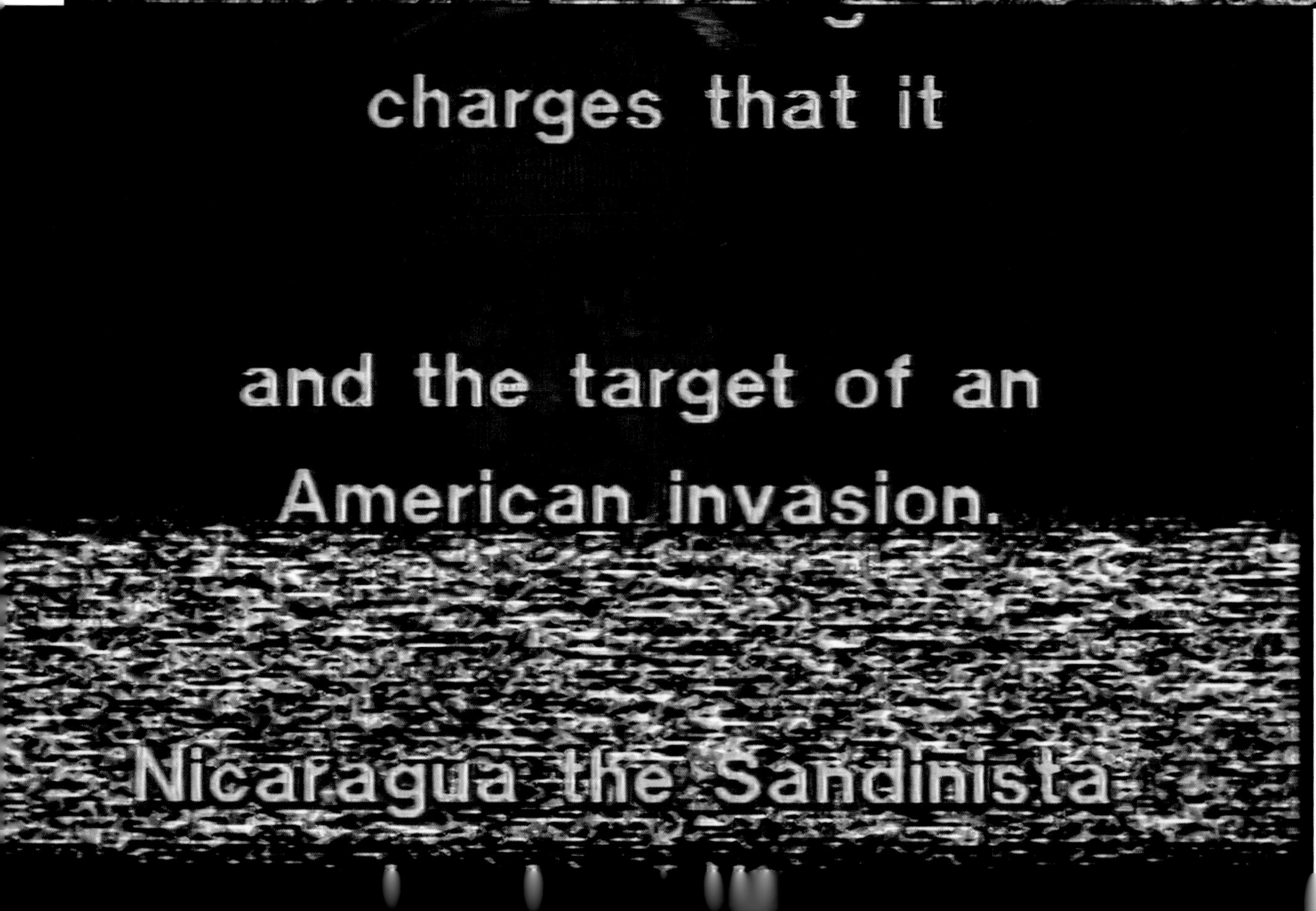
charges that it
and the target of an
American invasion.
Nicaragua the Sandinista

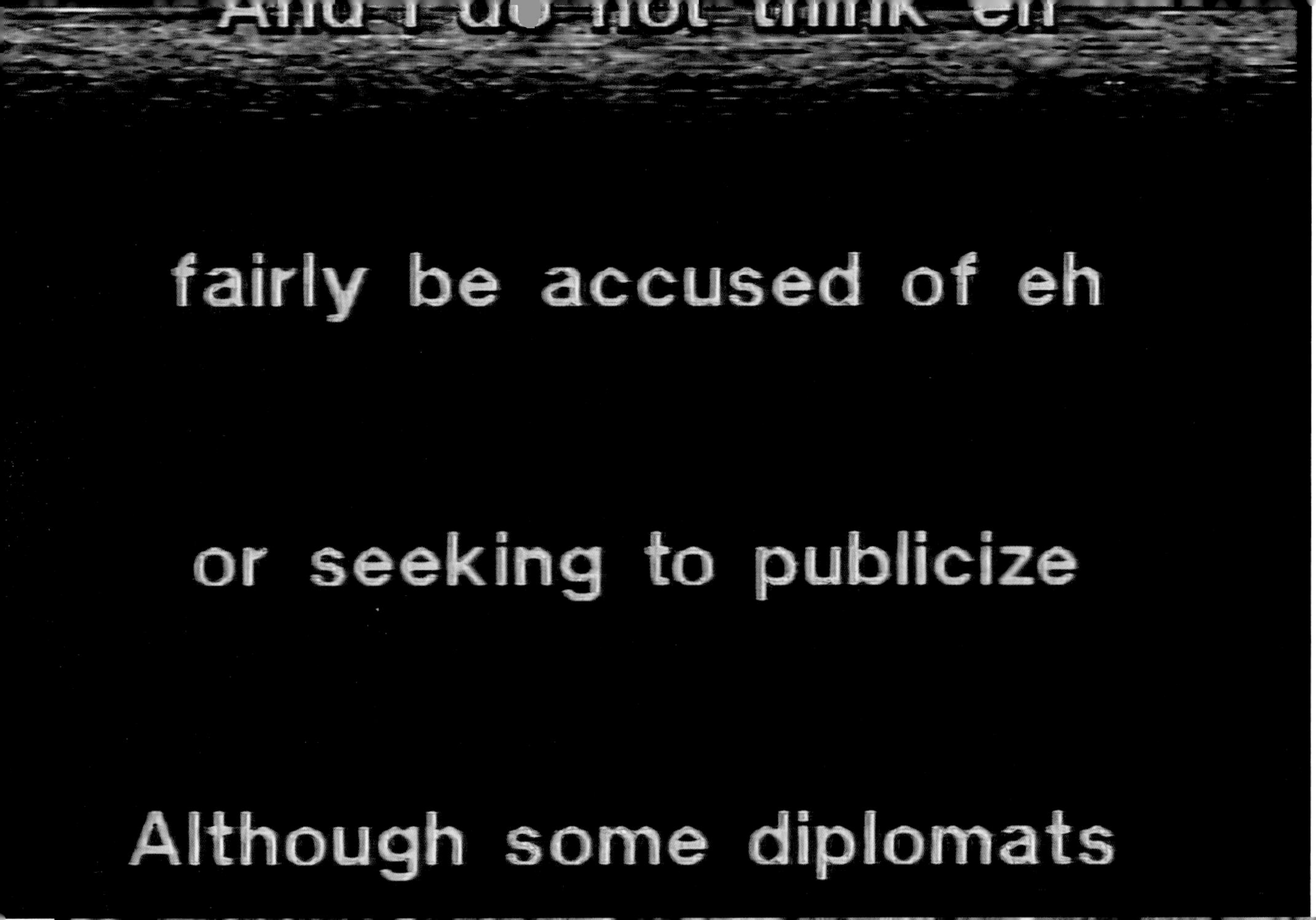

And I do not think eh

fairly be accused of eh

or seeking to publicize

Although some diplomats

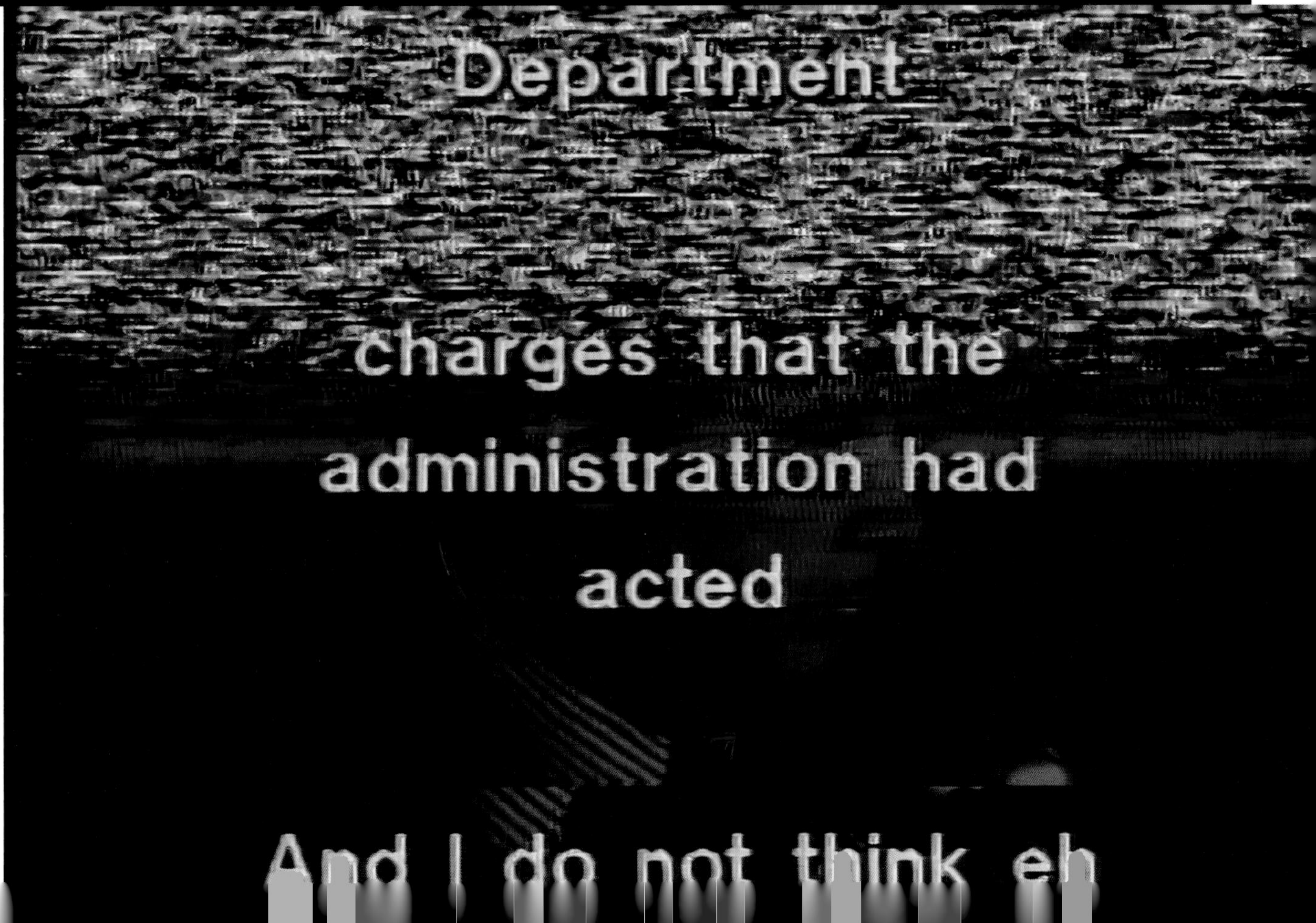

Department

charges that the
administration had
acted

And I do not think eh

**Black Audio Film Collective
(UK, active 1982–1998)
John Akomfrah
(British, born 1957)**

**HANDSWORTH SONGS. 1986
16mm film transferred to high-
definition video (color, sound),
58:33 min.**

Handsworth Songs is a close study of the rage that powered the 1985 riots in the Handsworth district of Birmingham, England. Race and class collide to set the scene, producing a spark that sets decades of imperial transnational relations alight. As the film splinters off in various thematic directions, conversations with members of British Caribbean and Sikh communities are interwoven with archival footage culled from the Archive Film Agency, the Birmingham Central Library, the BBC, and Pathé Film Library. The flow of interviews and historical scenes is punctuated by floating family portraits of Black Britons and slow pans across the *Guernica*-esque painting *The Dream, the Rumour and the Poet's Song*, a 1985 public mural depicting both the optimism and the brutality of the migrant experience. As the film progresses, the aspirations of the Windrush generation—Caribbeans who emigrated to the United Kingdom in the decades immediately after World War II—dissipate into the harsh realities of 1980s Britain. Images of state violence, racism, and neglect bleed into an unruly soundscape of reggae and punk.

Directed by John Akomfrah and produced by Lina Gopaul, the film was broadcast in July 1987 on the free public-service television network Channel 4 and only reentered the cultural zeitgeist in 2002, through its inclusion in the international art exhibition Documenta 11, organized that year by Okwui Enwezor.

It is a defining work of the Black Audio Film Collective, whose members, in addition to Akomfrah and Gopaul, included Reece Auguiste, Edward George, Avril Johnson, David Lawson, and Trevor Mathison, each of whom contributed to every stage of the production and dissemination of *Handsworth Songs*. Their collective claim to filmic possibility—moving beyond the auteur model—resulted in a film that is conceptually rangy and affectively porous. Yet, as the scholar Saidiya Hartman has noted, the terms of critique in the work are pointed. The aim is not only the end of state violence and anti-Black racism or the destitution of "a state founded on racial slavery and settler colonialism, attacking heteropatriarchy, reimagining species life." It is the application of "pressure on all of those fronts simultaneously"—with incendiary precision and sustained commitment. Old tricks of liberal inclusion or symbolic politics will not do. Instead, as the film's concluding phrases articulate, *Handsworth Songs* invites us to "bear witness to the process by which the living transforms the dead into partners in struggle."

OLUREMI C. ONABANJO

Tony Cokes
(American, born 1956)

BLACK CELEBRATION. 1988
Standard-definition video
(black and white, sound), 17:11 min.

Since the mid-1980s, Tony Cokes has been composing essay-istic multimedia installations that are more than the sum of their parts. Weaving together music, archival film footage, and critical theory, they investigate the ways in which media shape modes of civic and political protest. *Black Celebration* features newsreel footage of the riots that took place in Black neighborhoods across the United States in the 1960s—in sections of Boston, Newark, and Detroit, as well as the Watts area of Los Angeles—and intersperses it with text commentary. Replacing the original voice-overs with the pulsating music of industrial-rock group Skinny Puppy, and featuring texts by artist Barbara Kruger, musicians Morrissey and Martin Lee Gore (of Depeche Mode), and the revolutionary Situationist International, Cokes's iconic video radically repositions the footage, recoding imagery that historically has been used to denigrate rioters and present their uprisings as dangerous threats to the prevailing capitalist order.

The video unspools in a series of black-and-white shots of desolate streets, buildings engulfed in flames, and protest-ers under arrest by heavily armed police officers, a nonlinear sequence of scenes that echoes the Situationist concept of the *dérive*, or drift, an unstructured journey through the urban landscape. Cokes's interest in industrial pop music stems from

its relationship to labor and its origins in Southern plantation songs, with their inherent power of resistance. The soundtrack's additional deployment of noise, distortion, and enraged screaming, as well as what critic Mark Fisher has called "Duchamp-found sounds" and "audio-hallucinatory fragmentation," defies clear communication and prompts new readings of the familiar imagery.

Cokes is part of a community of Black filmmakers who came to prominence in the 1980s making work that responded to the repressive policing of Black communities, including the Black Audio Film Collective (*Handsworth Songs*, 1986) and Sankofa Film and Video Collective (*Who Killed Colin Roach?*, 1983), among others. Refuting the received idea that mass expressions of grievance are inherently lawless whenever Black people are involved, *Black Celebration*, Cokes has said, poses the question, "How do people make history under condi-tions pre-established to dissuade them from intervening in it?"

DANIELLE A. JACKSON

LETS HAVE A BLACK CELEBRATION

BLACK CELEBRATION TONIGHT

ALWAYS...KNOWS THE
PROSPECTS.

LEARN TO EXPECT...
NOTHING.

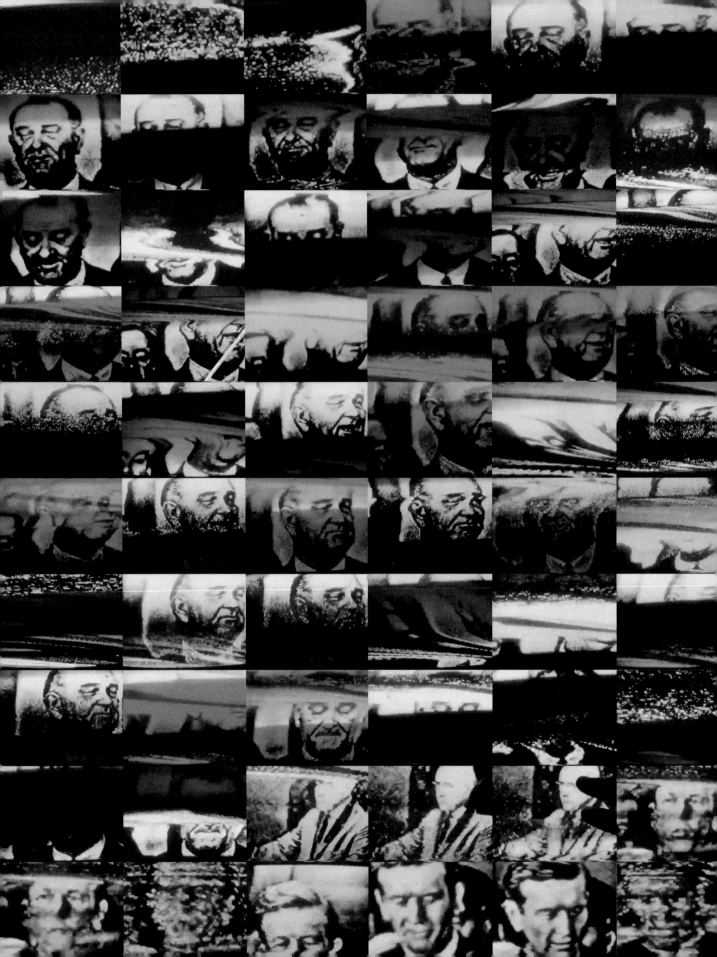

SPLIT SCREENS AND PARTITIONED PUBLICS
David Joselit

In *On Revolution*, Hannah Arendt makes a penetrating observation on the genealogy of the term *revolution*. Noting a shift from the Copernican meaning of the word—as the revolution of planets around the sun—to subsequent political adaptations in the seventeenth century, she recounts how, even in the latter context, it continued to signify a *return* rather than a *rupture*:

> In the seventeenth century, where we find the word [revolution] for the first time as a political term, the metaphoric content was even closer to the original [astronomical] meaning of the word, for it was used for a movement of revolving back to some pre-established point and, by implication, of swinging back into a preordained order. Thus, the word was first used not when what we call a revolution broke out in England and Cromwell rose to the first revolutionary dictatorship, but on the contrary, in 1660, after the overthrow of the Rump Parliament and at the occasion of the restoration of the monarchy. . . . The fact that the word "revolution" meant originally restoration, hence something which to us is its very opposite, is not a mere oddity of semantics. The revolutions of the seventeenth and eighteenth centuries, which to us appear to show all evidence of a new spirit, the spirit of the modern age, were intended to be restorations.[1]

Arendt's analysis allows us to rethink *revolution* in light of returns: a return is not the antithesis of a rupture; ruptures, small and large, are endemic to returns, and vice versa. Even in the context of the American Revolution, she argues, "[Thomas] Paine wanted no more than to recapture the old meaning of the word 'revolution' and to express his firm conviction that the events of the time had caused men to revolve back to an 'early period' when they had been in the possession of rights and liberties of which tyranny and conquest had dispossessed them."[2] In other words, the intention to return to a previous political state resulted in actions and events that created something new, a rupture. In our own time, this dynamic has reversed. Now it is typical for a stated revolutionary intention—an aim to rupture—to mask instances of historical or ideological return. An emphasis on rupture is evident in the history of Western modernism, which has been told as a syncopation of significant political revolutions and aesthetic breaks, conventionally beginning in eighteenth-century France and ending with the worldwide student movements of the 1960s; or beginning with Romanticism and ending with Conceptual art. But this is a narrative that tends to undervalue myriad aesthetic returns, including persistent allusions to classicism and frequent reanimations of academic realism. The inflation of the term *revolution* is, of course, most obvious in advertising, where ordinary products are credited with extreme novelty. In our current moment, then, the connotations of revolution are the reverse of what Arendt diagnosed with regard to the seventeenth century. Now revolution suggests a sequence of perpetual ruptures that serve to veil ideological returns.

Opposite Nam June Paik and Jud Yalkut. *Video Tape Study No. 3*. 1967–69/1992. Standard-definition video (black and white, sound), 4:01 min. The Museum of Modern Art, New York. Acquired through the generosity of Barbara Wise

1 Hannah Arendt, *On Revolution* (London: Penguin, 1963), 42–43.
2 Arendt, *On Revolution*, 45.

Because of its ubiquity as a term of value in art, commerce, and politics, and because of the significant shifts that have occurred in its meaning over the past five centuries, *revolution* must be rethought in terms of the shifting ratios it articulates over time between rupture and return.[3] With this goal in mind, I wish to engage two media formats that emerged between the 1960s and 1990s—the twenty-four-hour news cycle and political spin. These formats reconfigured the late-twentieth-century media ecology, not only prefiguring the format of the internet but also indirectly or directly engaging generations of video artists. The rotational—or "revolutionary"—format of the twenty-four-hour news cycle and the centrifugal drift of spin each establish a specific dialectic between return and rupture. The intended effect of both is to produce an atmosphere of absolute contemporaneity—of permanent rupture—in order to mask the actually existing stability of capitalist economies. For this they require perpetual breaks which, as I will argue, are afforded spatially by split screens and temporally by regular interruptions of breaking news. An experience of contemporaneity—of perpetual change—is thus arduously constructed from a constant rhythm of splitting and breaking that does little, if anything, to chip away at the neoliberal bedrock that grounds it. The fact that contemporaneity is *produced* is exemplified in Donald J. Trump's devastatingly effective media strategy in which one "wins the day" through creating an outrageous news story that dominates the twenty-four-hour cycle, then begins again the next day with a new storyline, as though from a tabula rasa, refusing to acknowledge (let alone apologize for) the previous day's media furor. Trump demonstrated that producing the contemporary is a process of permanent escalation within the twenty-four-hour media cycle, an eradication of history that paves the way for absolutism.

CYCLES

Beginning in the 1950s, the architecture of television developed into a stratified schedule of time blocks and program genres corresponding to different audiences—often identified by gender, age, and class. The television day was a complex rotation—a kind of narrative clock—that marked a diurnal progression from morning talk shows to midday soap operas, followed by after-school specials for children and adolescents, then the evening news, prime-time dramas and sitcoms, and late-night variety talk shows aimed exclusively at adults. As Raymond Williams argued in his 1974 book *Television: Technology and Cultural Form*, TV is best described not by analyzing its individual programs but by assessing the temporal flow it establishes throughout the day. Williams further recognized that in commercial television, such flows are not limited to the succession of programming alone but also encompass its intentional and regular interruption by advertising:

> It is now obvious, in both British and American commercial television, that the notion of "interruption," while it has still some residual force from an older model, has become inadequate. What is being offered is not, in older terms, a programme of discrete units with particular insertions, but a planned flow, in which the true series is not the published sequence of programme items but this sequence transformed by the inclusion of another kind of sequence, so that these sequences together compose the real flow, the real "broadcasting."[4]

3 This question of rupture's relation to return has a broader significance with regard to Eurocentric modes of history and their critique by postcolonial and Indigenous thinkers. While Western history (and art history) tends to proceed according to historicist models in which some kind of progress (or, at least, forward movement of time) is assumed, histories from the Global South and Native communities are premised on different kinds of relations or continuities between pasts, presents, and futures. Returns can be a resource for contemporary history, politics, and art. For my treatment of this issue with regard to global contemporary art, see my *Heritage and Debt: Art in Globalization* (Cambridge, MA: MIT Press/October Books, 2020).
4 Raymond Williams, *Television: Technology and Cultural Form* (1974; London: Routledge, 2003), 90–91.

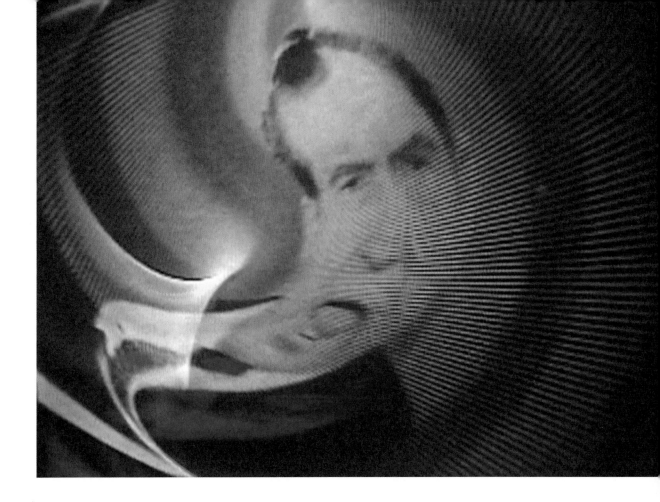

Above Nam June Paik. *Electronic Opera #1.* 1969. Standard-definition video (color, sound), 4:45 min. GBH Archives

In 1980, entrepreneur Ted Turner created the Cable News Network, or CNN, as a dedicated twenty-four-hour news channel, establishing a new format for televisual flow. In place of a succession of programmatic genres conforming to delimited time slots, CNN offered open-ended air time with the capacity to follow events as they unfolded, without temporal limits (and, given its devotion to satellite broadcasting, without spatial limits either). This relative dedifferentiation of temporal flow vis-à-vis programming genre corresponded to the network's ultimately successful effort to globalize its audience, as well as cable television's eventual adoption of narrowcasting as a norm. Despite the current dominance of such formats, it was not at all evident in 1980 that Turner's gambit would succeed. The former president of CBS news, documentary-television pioneer Fred Friendly, expressed skepticism: "Turner will show the promise, but he may not be able to deliver. He's the first man on the beach. Unfortunately, the first man on the beach rarely stays around to develop the colony."[5]

Friendly's metaphorical invocation of colonization, in which armed struggle is implicit, turned out to be prescient. CNN's viability was definitively confirmed in a moment of American neocolonial military action—the first Gulf War, in 1991. CNN, which had painstakingly negotiated with the Iraqi government for a satellite link, was the sole network capable of broadcasting the American bombardment of Baghdad on January 17, 1991, live from Baghdad. Even though the satellite feed was disabled after just sixteen hours, when Iraqi officials shut down the

5 Fred Friendly, quoted in Harry F. Waters et al., "Ted Turner Tackles TV News," *Newsweek*, June 16, 1980, 58.

phone lines, the footage was not only riveting but coveted by other networks and rebroadcast by them. War played into what one journalist called CNN's "unquenchable lust for the breaking story."[6] The paradox of such breaking stories, however, is that in order to sustain the affect of liveness, a live event requires many regular interruptions. This *breaking* of the live event—*breaking* news—is a form of internal rupture that ensures the effect of contemporaneity.[7] The breaks restart the clock, over and over again. In the end, few moments are as captivating as an actual bombardment, and much of a twenty-four-hour news cycle is uneventful, even outright boring; to counter this, breaks serve as renewed calls on the viewer's attention.[8] In 1991, *Newsweek* reported,

> As riveting as it was, the Gulf War was hardly made for television. Watching the procession of talking heads, political consultant John Buckley joked that Iraq's ancient city should be spelled "Babble-on." While the war was packaged almost like a mini-series and the attacks on Iraq and Israel both began conveniently in prime time, all of the satellite technology did nothing to speed the flow of real information. The military provided few briefings, most of which were virtually fact-free. Pool footage of the inaccessible air war was often 24 hours late.[9]

Rather than resembling a miniseries, however, CNN's war coverage had much more in common with the most prominent form of live television that preceded it—sports. Indeed, in the period leading up to the founding of CNN, the legendary ABC sports and news producer Roone Arledge had transformed live coverage from the standard perspective of a limited number of stationary cameras to a dynamic narrative full of suspense and audience identification, in which footage of athletes and coaches was edited to make them characters in a drama.[10] It is no coincidence that Arledge was subsequently tapped to run ABC's struggling news organization, in 1977, where he introduced many of the same narrative and aesthetic techniques. His 2002 obituary in *Variety* recounts,

> Under Arledge, sports coverage changed from static to kinetic— multiple cameras and sound recorders, handheld cameras to add immediacy and intimacy, reaction shots from the stands. He attached cameras to racing cars, boats and skis. Groundbreaking technical achievements included slow-motion and stop-action techniques, split screens and underwater cameras for sports such as diving. And, of course, the instant replay.[11]

CNN also became known for such techniques. In 1980, *Newsweek* reported that "Turner has equipped his troops with the most sophisticated hardware available, and the imaginative [CNN president Reese] Schonfeld plans to put it to intriguing use. A split-screen 'inset' device will keep watch on a developing story . . . while the scheduled program continues."[12]

In its capacity to show multiple developing stories simultaneously, the split screen is an effective means of providing the break in breaking news, and it has developed from an innovation in sports coverage and ultimately the twenty-four-hour news cycle to a term that is now commonly used to describe the deep divisions in American politics (and perhaps global politics as well). To put it bluntly, breaking news has had a significant role in breaking our polity. I want to consider how the split screen not only abets the mass production of contemporaneity that is the twenty-four-hour news cycle—which the rise of the internet has only

6 Dick Polman, "News without End," *Philadelphia Inquirer Magazine*, March 19, 1991, 27, quoted in Barbie Zelizer, "CNN, the Gulf War, and Journalistic Practice," *Journal of Communication* 42, no. 1 (Winter 1992): 72.

7 It is significant to recognize that this logic of interruption was noted by Williams in terms of commercials breaking into television shows. I think there is also an effect of liveness that is produced by this structure.

8 This structural breaking of an ostensibly continuous news cycle is taken up as an aesthetic device in Dara Birnbaum's 1990 video installation *Tiananmen Square: Break-In Transmission*, in which Birnbaum samples the diverse television coverage of the 1989 Tiananmen Square protests and also employs a "surveillance switcher" that grabs material at random from those channels and streams them on a fifth display. Distinct image flows generated from the same historical event are dispersed across monitors suspended within a gallery on specially designed supports attached to the ceiling. To put it simply, Birnbaum visualizes the temporal ruptures of the twenty-four-hour news cycle as a dispersion in space.

9 Jonathan Alter with bureau reports, "When CNN Hit Its Target," *Newsweek*, January 28, 1991, 41.

10 Perhaps it could be argued that sports was the first form of "reality TV," but to prove such a proposition is beyond the scope of this essay.

11 Richard Natale, "Roone Changed Rules of the Television Game," *Variety*, December 9–15, 2002, 71. See also Travis Vogan, *ABC Sports: The Rise and Fall of Network Sports Television* (Berkeley: University of California Press, 2018).

12 Waters, "Ted Turner Tackles TV News," 58.

Fig. 1 Joan Jonas. *Vertical Roll*. 1972. Standard-definition video (black and white, sound), 19:38 min. The Museum of Modern Art, New York. Acquired through the generosity of Barbara Pine

13 See my *Feedback: Television against Democracy* (Cambridge, MA: MIT Press, 2007).

14 David S. Broder, "Why Change Everything?," *Washington Post*, February 22, 1984. At my request, a Harvard research librarian made a search for the term used politically, and this was the earliest use she found in the *New York Times* or *Washington Post*, though she couldn't definitively identify a first use of the term. For my purposes, it is enough to note that *split-screen* arises as a political characterization by the mid-1980s and shifts in its valence and frequency of use along the lines that I trace.

15 Jeremy Gerard, "President Complains about TV's Use of Split Images," *New York Times*, January 6, 1990, 11. Ironically, it was reported in this article that Roone Arledge "called the broadcast control room and ordered the return to a full picture of the President. The ABC News anchor, Peter Jennings, explained to viewers that Mr. Bush did not know the technique was being used. . . . Through a spokesman . . . Mr. Arledge said yesterday that he agreed with the President's assessment."

16 Francine Kiefer, "Clinton Projects a 'Split-Screen' Presidency," *Christian Science Monitor*, January 19, 1999, 2.

17 See, for instance, John Haltiwanger, "Trump Created a Bizarre Split-Screen Moment by Holding a Campaign Rally in a Battleground State as the House Voted to Impeach Him," *Business Insider* (online), December 19, 2019.

accelerated—but also corresponds to the development of deeply fractured public spheres, where American citizens, for instance, can adopt entirely different worldviews depending on the news source they patronize. In these televisual publics, the split between screens functions as a firm boundary that the internet has multiplied as superimposed windows.

Among artists in the 1970s, the split had already migrated into the screen's interior. In Joan Jonas's single-channel tape *Vertical Roll* (1972), for instance, a rolling horizontal bar, caused by a common disfunction in the television signal, rhythmically punctuates the artist's performance, transforming her into a percussive body without organs (fig. 1). And Dan Graham's Time Delay Room installations of the mid-1970s, in which live video streams (on a short delay) were transmitted to adjacent rooms (thus feeding back a disorienting mix of images of a particular room's occupants and/or people like them in another room), established a different way of splitting a person from her representation. If the split screen in news separates balkanized events or self-possessed commentators, the split in early video occurs within an individual's perception of herself as an image: it is a split within the screen, between a person and "her" picture.[13]

While plausibly describing the same sort of alienation, these two kinds of splits—in television news and video art—have dramatically different politics. Video artists sought to destabilize the proprietary relationship between one's bodily experience and one's public representation. Television news, on the other hand, externalizes difference as an extreme form of political self-possession, as the evolution of *split screen* from a merely technical term in the 1950s to a political one in the 1980s demonstrates.

In 1984, journalist David S. Broder declared in the pages of the *Washington Post* that "there is a split-screen quality to the political dialogue at this time of year that is as vexing as it is inevitable. The spokesmen for the opposing parties are not so much debating as they are talking past each other."[14] It is worth noting here that split screens enable the proliferation of "spin," and it is the effects of spin that Broder points to when he suggests that opposing parties in a debate are "talking past each other." In 1990, American president George H. W. Bush discovered and decried the danger of a different kind of split screen. According to the *New York Times*, he "complained . . . that by juxtaposing pictures of him in a jocular mood during a news conference . . . and the arrival of the bodies of American soldiers killed in Panama, some television news organizations had made him appear insensitive to the deaths." In an index of how novel the now ubiquitous split-screen device was in 1990, Bush asked for warning from networks when they planned to use it: "I would respectfully request that if the urgency of the moment is such that such a technique is going to be used, if I could be told about it . . . and we'll stop the proceedings [of a news conference]."[15] Needless to say, the president's request was not honored by any network, and the use of the split screen as a technique for representing political contradiction had become widespread enough by the end of the 1990s for Bill Clinton's administration to be called a "'split-screen' presidency."[16] It is no coincidence that this characterization was made during Clinton's impeachment trial, when the president was working hard to give the impression that business was proceeding as usual in the White House. (Similarly, Trump's performance during his 2020 impeachment trial was often characterized as "split-screen."[17]) By 1999 the term had migrated from a noun denoting a rogue device, in the eyes of the first President Bush, to an adjective describing presidential spin. Ten years later, in 2019, a *New York Times* journalist transformed the adjective into a verb in an article titled "Who Can Split-Screen Trump?" The answer, the author suggested, was the Democratic presidential candidate Beto O'Rourke, who might have been able to upstage, or out-spin, Trump: "By holding a rally in Mr. O'Rourke's home base, the president gave him the chance to do what few political opponents have managed since 2015: to split-screen him."[18]

To split-screen someone is to contradict their message by eclipsing it with a different one. It means countering one version of reality with another or, in the notorious words of Trump Administration official Kellyanne Conway, with "alternative facts." This logic has now been institutionalized as a spectrum of news outlets that dispense dramatically different "factual" accounts. One clear example of this policy was the choice of the right-wing network Fox News on June 9, 2022, not to run the day's prime-time hearings on the January 6 insurrection at the US Capitol (itself an event that unfolded on live-streaming split screens around the world). Instead, a "split-screen" narrative was presented in an effort to discredit those hearings.[19] When set side by side and spun out in different directions, such contradictory media worldviews are meant to occlude rather than engage one another: they allow no space for dialogue. If Raymond Williams showed that the televisual day was broken down by genre in the mid-twentieth century, today it is divided by ideological conviction.

It is the violence of this split—which is both political and aesthetic—that Nam June Paik consistently addressed in his video installations and satellite art. In his various arrangements of monitors, whether scattered among houseplants in *TV Garden* (1974; fig. 2) or organized

18 James Poniewozik, "Who Can Split-Screen Trump?," *New York Times*, February 12, 2019.
19 See Jeremy W. Peters, "Fox News Gives Its Viewers a Revisionist History Lesson of Jan. 6," *New York Times*, June 9, 2022.

Fig. 2 Nam June Paik. *TV Garden*. 1974 (2000 version). Standard-definition video (color, sound; 29 min.), minimum of thirty television sets, and live plants, dimensions variable. Solomon R. Guggenheim Museum, New York. Purchased with funds contributed by the International Director's Council and Executive Committee Members and through prior gift of The Bohen Foundation, 2001

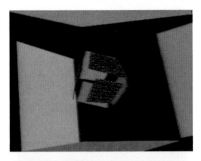

Figs. 3, 4 Nam June Paik. *Good Morning, Mr. Orwell.* 1984. Standard-definition video (color, sound), 38 min. Edited by Skip Blumberg. The Museum of Modern Art, New York. Gift of the artist. Fig. 4: Fireworks display by Jean Tinguely and Niki de Saint Phalle, Paris, with John Cage (inset)

20 Nam June Paik, "First Script for *Good Morning, Mr. Orwell*" (1983), in *We Are in Open Circuits: Writings by Nam June Paik*, ed. John G. Hanhardt, Gregory Zinman, and Edith Decker-Phillips (Cambridge, MA: MIT Press, 2019), 222, 225.
21 Nam June Paik, "Art & Satellite" (1984), in *We Are in Open Circuits*, 180.

in grids in later works such as *Fin de Siècle II* (1989), splits function as porous contact zones rather than inviolable borders: not only do streams of content migrate from monitor to monitor, crossing and recrossing the gaps that divide them, but the multiplication and distortion of internal frames and other effects within the video channels denaturalize or decenter the primacy of the split between monitors. This proliferation of internal divisions within video content and external divisions between monitors is generative rather than restrictive. The split, in other words, is a navigable space of interchange rather than a void or vacuum into which dialogue disappears. Paik attempted to bridge the split screen most explicitly in his live satellite projects of the 1980s, which exploited the technology that enabled CNN's instantaneous global broadcasts during the same period. The first of these, *Good Morning, Mr. Orwell* (1984), which linked New York and Paris live by satellite and also delivered broadcasts to Germany and South Korea—reaching twenty-five million viewers around the world—took place the same year Broder detected a "split-screen quality to the political dialogue" (figs. 3–6). In addition to a heterogenous series of performances by the likes of Laurie Anderson, Philip Glass, Oingo Boingo, Allen Ginsberg, and Joseph Beuys, in an early script Paik proposed such space-defying actions as "Merce Cunningham and Jean-Louis Barrault making a sky duet on live TV" and "Using the split-screen technique, I pour Amstel Beer to a cup held by John Cage (or somebody else) . . . trans-atlantically."[20]

While he didn't succeed in executing these particular actions, Paik found other ways to defy differences in time and space through the multiplication of internal screens, which tended to morph and transform, establishing an intercommunicating mosaic that created connections rather than foreclosing them. Paik's project, which was full of technical problems and limitations, was not capable of redressing the media landscape in the United States and elsewhere. Nonetheless, he went further than either Jonas or Graham in articulating how splits between screens (as social balkanization) and within screens (as subjective splitting between affect and image) can function as a site of encounter with otherness rather than a point of irreconcilable contradiction. As he eloquently stated in 1984,

> Satellite art . . . does not merely transmit existing symphonies and operas to other lands. It must consider how to achieve a two-way connection between opposites of the earth; how to give a conversational structure to the art; how to master difference in time; how to play with improvisation, in-determinism, echoes, feedbacks, and empty spaces in the [C]agean sense; and how to instantaneously manage the differences in culture, preconceptions and common sense that exist between various nations. Satellite art must make the most of these elements (for they can become strengths or weaknesses) creating a multitemporal, multispatial symphony.[21]

In his allusion to George Orwell, author of the dystopian novel *1984*, Paik sought to turn television's ideological uniformity—its association with Orwell's authoritarian, all-seeing Big Brother—against itself, precisely by using the split screen to mark geographical differences that could be bridged "diplomatically," as it were, by performers and avant-garde artists. Paik was visionary in treating television as though it were the internet—a multilateral network that literally spans the globe. What he could not know in 1984 was that the internet's capacity to bring people

NEW-YORK

PARIS

Fig. 7   Nam June Paik.
Electronic Opera #1. 1969

together would become simultaneously and inextricably joined to a regime of surveillance, disinformation, and division that has saturated the world. In today's media landscape, there is no satellite diplomacy without Big Brother listening in.

SPIN

Paik understood both the gravitational pull of images and their capacity to spin out of control; it is no coincidence that making images spin was one of his signature devices. He famously accomplished this by bending television signals with magnets or distorting them with the video synthesizer he developed with Shuya Abe in 1969. In other words, he subjected them to the same diversionary logic that political spin exerts on discourse: in works such as *Study I: Mayor Lindsay* (1965), *Video Tape Study No. 3* (1967–69), and *Electronic Opera #1* (1969), the faces of New York mayor John V. Lindsay, President Richard Nixon, and Attorney General John Mitchell are distorted into a spiral that suggests, in a kind of counterspin, that they are circling down an electronic drain (see page 91 and fig. 7).

One of the most persuasive accounts of *spin*'s genesis as a political term links it to the curveball in baseball. As Randall Rothenberg recounted in his 1996 article "The Age of Spin,"

> In the 1950s, *spin*, as a verb, was used synonymously with *deceive*. By the time it made an appearance in politics—in 1972, managers of John V. Lindsay's short-lived presidential campaign were already talking of "spinning" reporters—it had passed from negative to neutral, becoming shorthand for polishing the truth.
>
> Central to this semantic shift is the understanding that spin cannot be a demonstrable lie. "It's what a pitcher does when he throws a curveball," says William Safire, a professional spinner before he became a pundit and lexicographer. "The English on a ball causes it to appear to be going in a slightly different direction than it actually is."[22]

A lie flatly contradicts something collectively accepted as true. Spin, on the other hand, insinuates an alternate truth. Rather than annihilating facts, spin diverts them and consequently reinvents them, in a kind of rupture within return. This is why and how the split screen and spin emerge together, mutually establishing their conditions of possibility. For the existence of a single truth must be authorized, whether actively or passively, by most or all members of a particular public. But spin, in its proliferation of meanings, its epistemological drift, requires belief. Collective authorization of facts gives way to individualized forms of belief in one or another alternate reality that the landscape of the split screen enables. The philosopher Neil C. Manson has written,

> If people *assume*—and must assume—that others are cooperative, then the spin doctor herself doesn't have to do anything to *induce* the belief that she herself is being cooperative on any particular occasion. . . . However, even though she does not *induce* the false belief, she can be viewed as culpable for *failing* to indicate that she is being uncooperative and shaping her selection of facts in a self-interested way.[23]

What Manson makes clear is that the bad faith of the spin doctor requires the gullibility (or one could say the good faith) of a targeted public. Indeed, we might wonder if what Paik considered as participation might not be better understood as a form of belief—a belief that

22 Randall Rothenberg, "The Age of Spin," *Esquire*, December 1996.
23 Neil C. Manson, "Making Sense of Spin," *Journal of Applied Philosophy* 29, no. 3 (August 2012): 209–10.

the diversion of a video signal with a magnet, for instance, constitutes a genuine intervention in the closed circuit of corporate broadcast television. From our historical vantage point, it is hard not to be skeptical about such interactions. We have learned from the internet that "participation" very often means the fracturing of citizen engagement into a split-screen world of irreconcilable beliefs, a vertiginous environment of competing convictions rather than an evidence-based world in which genuine debate may occur among those with different opinions but a shared archive of facts. Each opinion now lives on its own screen, split from all the others. This helps to clarify the use value of the arduous production of contemporaneity in which CNN and other news networks engage. Relentless contemporaneity evacuates the past and a concomitant sense of history, making way for new kinds of belief in "alternative facts." In this regard, there is something ominous about the dead metaphor of the "newsfeed." It is beyond doubt that propaganda is as old as human society, but we now *live on it* like nourishment—or a drug—checking our feeds countless times a day, never really knowing for certain if the information we're receiving comes from a reliable source or a malicious bot.

Paik's calls for audience participation in transforming the discursive structures of video and television may seem invalid, even quaint, at a moment when the internet—as the participatory medium par excellence—has proven itself an effective weapon of disinformation and hate. But his work on television has accomplished something crucially important. It makes us conscious of the affective materiality of our presumably dematerialized digital worlds. The capacity to play video like an instrument, as Paik did with his synthesizers and other tools, and

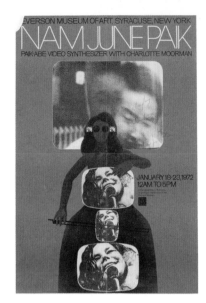

Fig. 8 Poster for the exhibition *Nam June Paik: Paik-Abe Video Synthesizer with Charlotte Moorman*, Everson Museum of Art, Syracuse, New York, 1972

as Charlotte Moorman did in the video cello he made for her (fig. 8), establishes a practice that is significantly different from bland audience participation: it is durational in a way distinct from the relentless liveness of television. *Playing* can be a synonym for *spinning*: to play someone can mean to deceive them. But playing video as one plays an instrument requires the creative intervention of a body that co-constitutes the informational signal. From early on, Paik introduced the body—his own, those of others, or the surrogate corpora of robots—into his works as a form of media. In *Listening to Music through the Mouth* (1962–63), he "ate" a record-player stylus, absorbing the sonic vibrations orally rather than aurally (fig. 9); in 1962's *Zen for Head* (fig. 10), Paik dragged his body loaded with ink like a human brush across a piece of paper laid on the floor, in an interpretation of La Monte Young's *Composition 1960 #10 (to Bob Morris)* (1960), whose score reads, "Draw a straight line / and follow it."

Engaging the body is precisely what other forms of mediated communication rigorously avoid. Disinformation, trolling, and viral attacks can all take place from a safe distance; the body of the active agent, as well as the necessary hardware, is out of range of the consequences. Paik's video art is a form of body art in which the ethical questions posed by being at once a human, an image, and a generator of images cannot be suppressed. Like Jonas and Graham in the 1970s, with their bodily interruptions of the supposedly frictionless, immaterial flow of media transmission—and also like contemporary artists such as Arthur Jafa and Martine Syms, who, in a different time and in distinctly different ways, explore both the mediation and repression of Black bodies in communications technology—Paik has performed digital splitting as an inscription in flesh, an electronic tattoo in the sensorium, that lingers past the next break.

Fig. 10 Nam June Paik performs
Zen for Head at Fluxus Internationale
Festspiele Neuester Musik, Städtisches
Museum, Wiesbaden, Germany,
September 1962

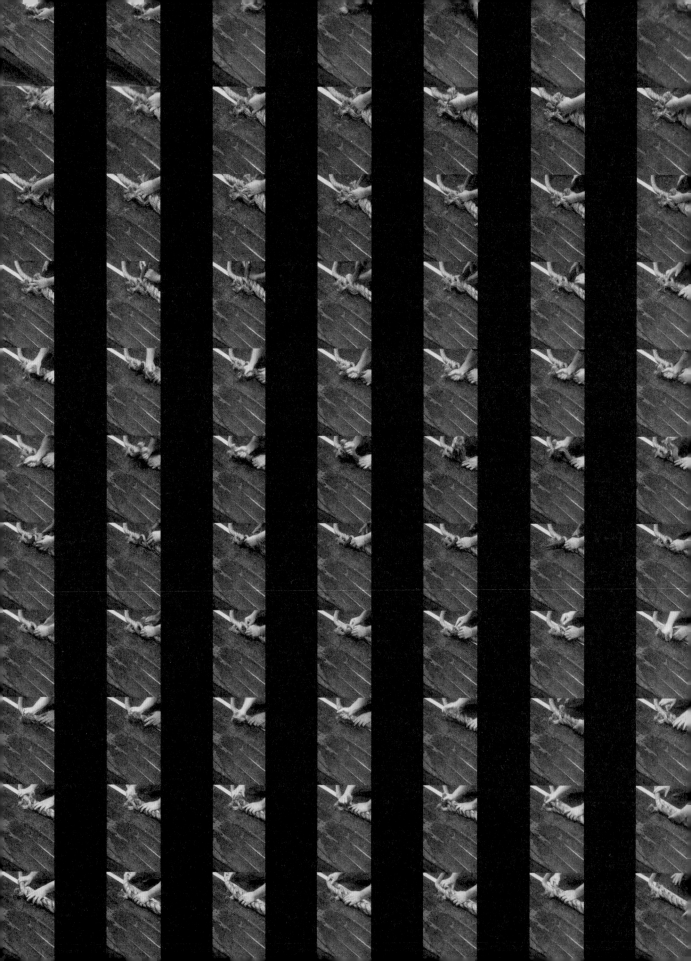

NEVER REST/UNREST: EMERGING TIME
Tiffany Sia

Artist Tiffany Sia's Never Rest/Unrest *(2020) is an on-the-ground account of the Hong Kong protests of 2019. Here Sia talks about this fraught experience, her use of hand-held iPhone video, and the politics and poetics of bearing witness to—and being embedded within—a period of social change.*

I shot *Never Rest/Unrest* between June and December 2019, during the most intense months of the Hong Kong protests. I was volunteering, shooting hundreds of hours of video footage, and *Never Rest/Unrest* was made alongside that. Video transmissions were the galvanizing force and connective tissue for each day of protest. There was a direct relationship between what was broadcast, what was shared and networked between screens, and what motivated people to assemble into this collective force. Images on social media and in broadcasts about assaults and beatings of protesters by police—that material drove the anger and fueled the fire. These relationships with screens constructed a new kind of public.

The smartphone affords a view of the front lines anywhere in the world, in any crisis and sometimes in real time. Anyone with a phone could have shot *Never Rest/Unrest*. This is the democratization of video, and it's happening at an unprecedented scale. It's a mass medium in which we are all literate, that we all intimately know. It is also how we see—we see through our screens. Millions of people are staring at their screens right now. That simple fact will never make headlines, it will never be the subject of History with a capital H, but it's crucial to think about how people interact with their screens. Networks of screens and the networked circulation of images have been intrinsic to twenty-first-century social movements, from the Arab Spring to the Umbrella Movement to the George Floyd uprisings. These movements were catalyzed by digital feeds and timelines, and organized through them.

Never Rest/Unrest takes up this new media vernacular, unlinking it from its networked context, and considers the vertical 16:9 video for its unique format. It is ubiquitous, everyday, and because of that it is also a medium you can disappear in: when you're filming from your phone on the street, you don't stand out. Moreover, as the filmmaker/protagonist of the work, I'm almost entirely unseen. I appear in only one frame. Other people are indicated by shadows and backs of heads in a relatively anonymized mass, and the viewer isn't permitted to see the most dangerous moments—those in which I or other subjects might be implicated, or our identities revealed. So the film takes on a ghostly aspect. Markers of context are omitted. The work also has no subtitles, so you're forced to sink into the sound and the images, to try to interpret what's happening. If you don't understand Cantonese, the film holds you at a distance. Protest chants repeat, but to pick up the patterns you have to be attentive. Language aside, raw emotion can be heard in people's voices. Indignance. Sometimes joy. The tactic was to show seemingly banal, insignificant scenes that suggest the relentlessness of everyday habitual resistance and the invisible spirit of the movement, of this particular moment of history making.

Pictures of the events in Hong Kong were restricted globally, but in the city spectacularly violent images were splashed on newspapers and all over our internet feeds. In contrast, I tried to create something

Opposite and following pages
Tiffany Sia. *Never Rest/Unrest*. 2020. High-definition video (color, sound), 29 min. The Museum of Modern Art, New York. Fund for the Twenty-First Century

anti-spectacular, against the spectacle of unrest, because what are the ethics of displaying those scenes? What narratives, both national and geopolitical, do they serve? This is the crux of the work's title. From the outside, people saw "unrest," but on the inside it was a period of "never resting." Inside, you wouldn't necessarily say, "We're in a period of unrest." That word implies a kind of distance or objectivity; it comes from a journalistic lexicon. People living through the events instead describe a complex process of political and psychological transformation. Resistance is folded into everyday life, fermenting in the ordinary. I was trying to show that experience visually through moving images—a medium in which no single image can be authoritative. The sequence of images builds to trace something total, something unnameable, about living through such a time.

Many shots in the film are driven by the ubiquity of screens and monitors throughout the city. They're on people and in the subways. They're all around you, showing advertisements, news broadcasts, video uploaded by citizen journalists or anonymous internet accounts. Between ads, news, and social media, it's an ambient culture of screens. What do they show, and what do they not show? How long will they show what they are showing now? Digital and broadcast material actively changes and adapts to new political conditions, in anticipation and in fear of censorship. These shifts—both seismic and coded—point to a certain temporality: the growing appearance of the illicit, the emergence of the concealed.

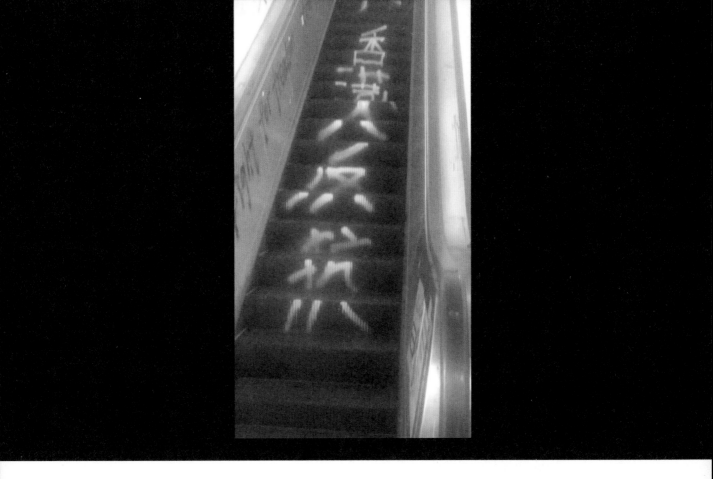

This is why *Never Rest/Unrest* avoids the immediacy of social media. The images lag. Although some sequences could be confused with Instagram Stories—they're unremarkable and disappear formally into "nothing"—they are far from instantaneous in their broadcast. The social aspects are connoted, but the images are reengineered—they're belated in relation to "real time," circulated differently. Still, the work uses the tempo of vernacular video and social media, and it's critical that it feels ordinary. It is inspired by Julio García Espinosa's manifesto "For an Imperfect Cinema," from 1969, in which he calls for a political cinema that embraces readily available mediums and less polished forms. "Art will not disappear into nothingness," he writes. "It will disappear into everything."[1] It is exactly in its ordinariness that *Never Rest/ Unrest* aims to show how time is experienced in prolonged moments of revolt, how people really experience historical shifts. The ubiquity of screens and their changes over time, the escalator that unfolds like an accordion to show a protest phrase inscribed on the steps: these unspectacular gestures are embedded in daily life.

This form of nonfiction storytelling is different from both propaganda and broadcast news. Those genres share formal qualities; they're intrinsically linked, either in conflict or working together. Do they tell us what's happening, or do they coerce us with their violent spectacles? Who is telling the story, and who can co-opt it? Social documentary films often use the same intensely emotional material—even when countering propaganda or state denialism. I am hyperaware of

1 Julio García Espinosa, "For an Imperfect Cinema" (1969), in *Film Manifestos and Global Cinema Cultures: A Critical Anthology*, ed. Scott MacKenzie (Berkeley: University of California Press, 2014), 230.

beyond them? Banal moments present another option; they're interesting because they're incontestable. In *Never Rest/Unrest*, I was trying to avoid adjudicating my position or attempting to persuade the viewer. The film is not about proof. It's not about evidence. It's not a plea. It's about life and endurance and the everyday.

Never Rest/Unrest is also an extremely intimate look into my life. You see my home, my commute. There are many things you could parse from the film to assemble a person . . . and the person is me. But you know that in making the film, I consented to this. It can happen the other way, when someone records someone else and then that person is exposed. What responsibility does the filmmaker have to that person? When capturing someone on film is an act of violence, the filmmaker joins the state in a surveillance practice (apropos of Catherine Zimmer's "surveillance cinema"). As a filmmaker, how can you defy that? How can you reject the gaze of the surveillance state? In *Never Rest/Unrest*, the only person I willingly expose is myself. The film does not have a distinct protagonist; it is not myself, the city, or even the people I'm with. The protagonist is more spectral—an atmosphere, a zeitgeist, a discrete, unnameable force that I as filmmaker am barely keeping pace with.

I was thinking about the ethics of documentation: what it means as evidence, but also the role of journalism in relation to historical change, to crisis. If documentation is an accumulation of evidence designed to hold certain powers accountable, we have to acknowledge that in many instances documentation already exists—and yet there is no justice. As artists, we have to ask what our motivations are in producing work with this kind of material. Why are we fetishizing indexicality and forensics?

Even in the process of litigation, this material retraumatizes victims. When using documentation as aesthetic material, are we posing the right questions? In what ways do we do the work of the state, even in making work that aims to resist the state?

In *Never Rest/Unrest*, I'm attempting to articulate a nonfiction form that integrates fugitivity, solidarity, and a more embodied gaze. I am thinking beyond documentation. The goal was to assemble another kind of vernacular for telling these stories. I knew that I would forget many of the moments I was recording—they were too insignificant to remember. But the banal scenes build a texture, they make up what feels so important about that time. What did it feel like during the fall of Rome? I was trying to get at a very elusive thing, to create a film that shows you as best it can the nothingness that is the process of history. Memory is crucial when history is being erased and reauthored by the state as part of a program of violence.

I just revisited Shu Lea Cheang's video installation *Making News/Making History: Live from Tiananmen Square* (1989). In one scene, the students are singing the national anthem. I think that's telling: they felt that it was patriotic to imagine a China in which they themselves could participate, even as the state deemed their fight for democracy—or, literally translated, "people's rule"—as threatening, motivated by foreign influence. No one really talks about that. That fact of that singing of the national anthem—with its repeating chorus of *Qiánjìn* (前进), "Enter into the front"—complicates the national memory, the state narrative that by now has been naturalized, transformed into history. It reminds us, as James C. Scott writes in *Seeing Like a State*, that "none of the historical participants in, say, World War I or the Battle of the Bulge, not to mention the Reformation or the Renaissance, knew at the time that they were participating in anything that could be so summarily described."[2]

Harun Farocki and Andrei Ujică's *Videograms of a Revolution* (1992) looks at this tension between history and memory. It examines the image trail of an event—the Romanian Revolution—through the medium of television. The 4:3 aspect ratio became obsolete in the 1990s in some countries and in the 2000s in others, so the work feels nostalgic, but the social conditions were actually very similar to today. *Videograms* tells us something important about video making around historical cusps or media events. We can see it as a process of real historiography, the conscious sorting and assembling of primary and secondary accounts.

I wasn't aware of all this while shooting *Never Rest/Unrest*, but I was later, when I began assembling the material. During my months of volunteering, I often thought about what it means to show images of violence. How much do those spectacles tell us about events? And how much do they obscure what's actually going on? I started shooting basically not wanting to spend through my SD cards. I didn't necessarily know that I was making a film, which might explain why the images feel unconscious, non-narrative. The scenes being depicted are constantly disappearing. I shot all the video in the moments of waiting—waiting for the cops to show up, waiting for something to happen—and so it captures the constant roil of anticipation, never knowing exactly when you are at the center of the event. A documentary film might give the impression that it's affording you a view of the center, the center of history, the center of a story. But what is the center? It always eludes you. Your arrival is imperceptible. You constantly ask yourself, am I there?

It seems so obvious after the fact, once historians or the news cycle have crystallized the narrative. Today, the memeability of a video

2 James C. Scott, *Seeing Like a State: How Certain Schemes to Improve the Human Condition Have Failed* (New Haven, CT: Yale University Press, 1998), 160.

may determine which narrative is at the center, which narrative is the victor. There's a huge gap between people's understanding of how they live through events—lived time—and this other more sanitized, linear, official time. *Never Rest/Unrest* asks how we could articulate a video vernacular of lived time. How do you trace time? Real time, dead time, historical time, everyday time . . . Time as depicted in the film might be hard to interpret, but it achieves a verisimilitude that cannot be accomplished through traditional narrative. The danger is that the work might be illegible; it is so banal in form and feeling, so ubiquitous in its aesthetic. But it attempts a kind of honesty, a vulnerability, in articulating this particular experience of time in Hong Kong.

The last scene of *Never Rest/Unrest* shows the 1997 ceremony in which control of Hong Kong was transferred from the United Kingdom to China. Does that ceremony represent the transformation of sovereignty, does it actualize it? Implicit in the handover scene is the knowledge that symbolic transformation is made material in the broadcast event. The rest of the film, the accumulation of ordinary but significant moments, suggests the ways in which political change accrues beyond highly ritualized televised political pageants. The lived transformation of sovereignty emerges beyond the frame, between sequences.

You could say that the crisis of war is defined by images of combat. But what about a legal crisis? What about a crisis of sovereignty, or a crisis of the rule of law? These are a challenge to image making; they evade capture. They're about duration of activity and the ways that activity smuggles itself in plain sight into bureaucracy and ordinary life. That is the very texture of authoritarianism. Its power is its ability to smuggle itself into the everyday. Violent images might obscure these other, subtler types of violence: the crisis festering in bureaucracy, the slow turn, the machinations. When you see images of violence, you feel a certain set of emotions: horror, pity, sympathy. But dread is what you feel when you can't see the horrifying scene. It's adjacent to horror, and it anticipates horror. Dread is not being able to see around the corner or over the horizon, and it defines so much of contemporary life and contemporary history. While we experience some moments of horror, there are exponentially more moments in which dread is the presiding feeling. This brings us back to the struggle to capture the true temporality of events and the importance of attending to minor registers of time.

Some people read *Never Rest/Unrest* as hopeful, but I think it simply shows bursts of hope, or glimmers, and even those are open to interpretation. Take, for example, the children singing a protest song in a shopping mall. The scene might seem hopeful, but it is also incredibly scary, given that the kids could have been arrested. Why are nine-year-olds protesting? Why are they so energized? How do they relate to this historical moment? They're all in their school uniforms, and their parents probably don't even know they're there. This is pre-pandemic, but they're wearing masks. How did they know to cover their faces, to hide their identities? Why, as children, are they afraid of being doxxed? The image creates a swell of feeling: first optimism, then something more sinister, even dread.

I showed *Never Rest/Unrest* publicly in Hong Kong once, in a secret screening at a university, a sort of surprise for the students. It was three months after the implementation of the national security law, and they all looked terrified. Some obviously didn't know how to react. They were probably thinking, am I supposed to be seeing this in school?

It might be difficult to watch the film if you're too close to the events. It could be impossible to see the images. But that is what's

interesting about them. They are unconscious images. Evan Calder Williams proposed "shard cinema" as a defining aesthetic of our era; *Never Rest/Unrest* offers "smudge cinema." In certain shots, you feel like you're a body in a crowd. You can see where the lens is smeared with oil from my fingers and the humidity in the air that enshrouds the image in a glow. The way the phone moves, the handheld device . . . It's an embodied gaze, and the film's relation to the body is in those traces.

A real material power—and danger—of video is its ability to incriminate its subjects. In capturing events, can artists and filmmakers create a new vernacular, an alternative to narratives of power? What's left of the artist's role to speak for the political or the contemporary? What's political about political film if material evidence is not enough to challenge the state? Participating in the surveillant aspects of filmmaking, exposing subjects and participants, and taking on the language of propaganda feel like a dead end. As an artist, I think we can, and must, demand more—from film, from nonfiction, and from narrative. We live within systems of impunity, and yet how we survive, sustain, feel, think, and think together produces a new poetics of power. That, for me, is the critical space.

As told to Stuart Comer, Lina Kavaliunas, and Michelle Kuo

PIRATE MEDIA
Ravi Sundaram

While most histories of video and television have focused on Western, large-scale, corporate broadcasting, Ravi Sundaram has explored the radical proliferation of low-cost video, bootlegged content, and pirate channels around the world beginning in the 1980s. The scholar calls this condition "pirate modernity," and it is key to understanding the recent history of media art in the Global South—and the video coursing through our interplanetary networks in the present.

When low-cost video arrived in the Global South in the 1980s, it sent shock waves through the region. Walter Benjamin famously used the metaphor of shock to describe the encounters of urban populations with the new technology of cinema in the 1920s—which "burst this prison-world asunder by the dynamite of the tenth of a second"[1]; the emergence of video in India and other nations created a similarly radical disturbance that continues to this day. Video- and audiocassettes circulated via nonlegal and informal networks, neighborhood shops, and bazaars, bypassing the control systems set up by large media corporations and governments. Existing systems of copyright and distribution were dramatically challenged. This was the context for the development of what I have called pirate modernity, a gray zone between urban informality and emergent media techniques. While pirate modernity produced radical conditions of insubordination in the South, it also drew subaltern populations into the networks of global media industries and addictive cycles of speculative desire.

At that moment in the 1980s, when video started expanding worldwide, it was understood as the memory of cinema or the memory of television. Then it very clearly became much more. It began to act. Video initiated new processes and new forms of memory that were reordered quite dynamically, and, most crucially, it anticipated a different set of publics.

From the very outset, video was also a technological process of sensing the world. The informal nature of early video in the non-Western world framed a leaky, proliferating technological sensorium, moving proprioception beyond the world of individual media objects. In every sense, I think, the emergence of video subverted and permanently incapacitated the postcolonial model of the social. Postcolonial regimes like India had partitioned the social from the medial, and welfare from desire, while carefully regulating public expression. This approach couldn't survive the storms initiated by video. In *Publics and Counterpublics* (2002), Michael Warner writes about the productive perversity of media publics, in that they typically overflow attempts at designation and control. By 2000, with the infrastructures of video piracy and informal distribution, censorship had become difficult. The hierarchies of cultural production were disturbed.

With video, technosocial milieus actively transform the meanings of political and cultural expressions. Video multiplies space-times, driving what Mark Hansen calls a "feed-forward" temporality of digital media, beyond human perception. Video shapes atmospheric infrastructures, which periodically draw new populations into media experiences, from ambient networks to everyday screen culture; media has become the infrastructural condition of life. Debates in the West have looked at video's signaletic nature and agency—its signifying capacity, the shift from the semiotic and representational, the relationship to television and cybernetic designs of feedback. In the Global South, the expressive capacity of this video-driven, post-postcolonial sensory infrastructure is unparalleled. In India, for example, unlike in

Opposite CAMP. *From Gulf to Gulf to Gulf.* 2013. High-definition video, standard-definition video, and cell-phone videos (color, sound), 83 min.

1 Walter Benjamin, "The Work of Art in the Age of Mechanical Reproduction," in *Illuminations: Essays and Reflections*, ed. Hannah Arendt, trans. Harry Zohn (New York: Schocken, 1968), 236.

the West, video technologies emerged simultaneously with the expansion of television, driven by a pirate infrastructure and growing cities.

In India—as in most parts of the world now—the experience of media has challenged our understanding of perception, which was once seen as unique to human experience. Now machines perceive, too: machine intelligence and network power are creating new sensations of simultaneity along with psychic instabilities. Video has produced microtemporal events that exceed human perception and animate different bodies of affect. In the early decades of video, pirate infrastructure played a crucial role in changing both human and technological modes of perception. Apart from disrupting copyright regimes, the circulatory energy of pirate aesthetics affected and disaffected publics and audiences, creating new forms of public perception and experience at a vastly greater scale. As a larger infrastructure of sensing, video mobilized a range of practices, from everyday pirating and bootlegging in working-class neighborhoods to Hindu nationalists deploying videocassettes. Moreover, video shaped emerging documentary filmmakers and a new generation of younger artists.

As a signaletic technology, video gave rise to a circulation engine with unfolding effects and multiple associations: political aesthetics, proletarian media infrastructures, and art practices. Unlike celluloid, which was contained by regulation and censorship, video set up multiple pathways with low thresholds of entry. Ina Blom has persuasively argued that video is not just a technology but a "form of agency" that

Fig. 1 Raqs Media Collective. *Co-Ordinates of Everyday Life, or, 28°28' N/77°15' E: 2001/2002.* 2002. Installation with video, audio, prints, stickers, and broadsheet. Detail view of multiscreen projection, Documenta 11, Kassel, Germany, 2002

2 Ina Blom, *The Autobiography of Video: The Life and Times of a Memory Technology* (Berlin: Sternberg, 2016).
3 Brian Larkin, "The Politics and Poetics of Infrastructure," *Annual Review of Anthropology* 42, no. 1 (2013): 327–43.

Fig. 2 "Check under your seat. There may be a bomb. Who is the stranger next to you?" Sticker from *Co-Ordinates of Everyday Life, or, 28°28′ N/77°15′ E: 2001/2002* (2002), by Raqs Media Collective, Documenta 11, Kassel, Germany, 2002

Fig. 3 Amar Kanwar. *The Torn First Pages*. 2004–08. Nineteen-channel standard-definition video (black and white and color, sound and silent; varying durations), nineteen sheets of paper, three metal frames, books, magazines, and artist books, dimensions variable. The Museum of Modern Art, New York. Acquired through the generosity of The Estate of Byron R. Meyer, Kiran Nadar of Kiran Nadar Museum of Art, and The Contemporary Arts Council. Installation view, Deutsche Guggenheim Museum, Berlin, 2010

Fig. 4 Amar Kanwar. *The Torn First Pages*. 2004–08. Still from *The Bodhi Tree* (2005)

shapes machine and human capacities.[2] It was always more than the work of individual artists or a proliferating culture of screens. Video initiated a set of radical individuations that foregrounded the general environmentality of media in everyday life.

Artists in India began to engage with video technology in the 1990s. Given the weakness of museums and other cultural institutions, pirate infrastructures dynamized video art practices as artists gained access to the archives of world cinema and video art. *Bombay/Mumbai 1992–2001*, organized by Geeta Kapur and Ashish Rajadhyaksha, drew connections between urbanism and video culture; it was one section of the widely seen 2001 Tate Modern exhibition *Century City: Art and Culture in the Modern Metropolis*. Curator Okwui Enwezor's Documenta 11, mounted in 2002, brought about an important shift. Framed by debates around postcolonialism, the exhibition went well beyond its original design. As an archive of the new diverse, low-cost infrastructure, Enwezor's project both anticipated and gave expression to a whole new conversation about art and its generative infrastructure, which was makeshift and profound, sharply conceptual and innovative, and refreshingly international. As Brian Larkin argues, infrastructures have a poetics: they can implode and make possible radical forms of transmission.[3]

The Indian artists in Documenta 11 were representative of the expanded technosocial milieu unleashed by video in the 1990s. For example, the multiscreen installation *Co-Ordinates of Everyday Life, or, 28°28′ N/77°15′ E: 2001/2002*, by Raqs Media Collective, featured a main-screen projection showing scenes of everyday life in the city, including imagery of trains changing tracks, working-class bicycle riders, accidents, displacement, and vibrant disorder (fig. 1). A floor projection presented a GIS (Geographic Information System) map newly introduced by the Indian state, while a text history of the legal expropriation of urban land played on another screen. Stickers made for display around Kassel provided a ludic interruption in the urban delirium (fig. 2).

After Documenta 11, video no longer merely represented social processes but became a form of active intervention in technosocial formations. "Video" was now less a format and more a mode of elastic expression. Amar Kanwar's *The Torn First Pages* is indicative of this turn. The installation, made between 2004 and 2008, references the Burmese bookseller Ko Than Htay, who defied the nation's military regime by removing mandatory ideological slogans—always printed on the first page—from the books he sold. Projected onto sheets of paper, a series of short videos present archival footage, still images, and fluid archival traces, evoking the turbulent temporality of the Burmese struggle for democracy (figs. 3, 4). In its use of intermedia installation and recursive critique, *The Torn First Pages* creates a unique sensory experience, bringing together politics and aesthetics via an interweaving of video, literature, and sculpture. Produced after Documenta 11 but before the expansion of social media, the work is remarkably intermedial, with its moving still images, found footage, memory making, and forensic or evidentiary forms of memory. Here video is a form of emergence, articulating a political aesthetics that goes beyond traditional formats.

I think this hybrid quality really comes to the fore in the projects of the Mumbai-based collective CAMP. In their 2013 video *From Gulf to Gulf to Gulf*, CAMP follows local ships and sailors across the Indian Ocean to Somalia, Yemen, the United Arab Emirates, Iran, Pakistan, and Western India (fig. 5). Using multiple formats, including low-resolution video generated by sailors on Nokia phones, VHS videocassettes, and high-definition video, the work addresses infrastructures of circulation

Fig. 5 CAMP. *From Gulf to Gulf to Gulf*. 2013.

as well as the environmental media aesthetics of the sea. For the multi-screen "city symphony" *In Cameras Res* (2019), CAMP manipulated and edited the footage from three automated CCTV cameras in Amsterdam, creating precise interventions into the all-seeing eyes of mechanized surveillance (figs. 6, 7). In 2007, the group cofounded the Public Access Digital Media Archive, or Pad.ma, an online archive of video and other digital documents. Objects in Pad.ma—including primary footage, resources from collectives, and artist- and activist-driven material—are densely annotated, and the collection is searchable and viewable online. The archive offers an alternative to models of algorithmic curation. It also takes seriously the intermedial questions posed by video. It's a post-video archival design, a way to navigate the feed-forward temporality of India's political environment, which makes public expression very difficult.

More than 80 percent of the data on the internet is video. Machines are now managing networks, vast numbers of people are involved, and specific body parts are engaged. Video is activating all kinds of vital energies—both of the body and of various side infrastructures. In this sense, what happened in the 1980s and what's happening today are not unconnected. Among the familiar manifestations are the lightness of the infrastructures, the attachment to these infrastructures of new populations and new actors, the mobilization of events, and the creation of new events.

Figs. 6, 7 CAMP. *In Cameras Res*. 2019. Three-channel high-definition video (color, silent) captured by automated 4K CCTV cameras, 20 min. Installation view, De Appel, Amsterdam, 2019

In recent years, video has been characterized by a fluid topology. Rather than a chronological move from analog to digital, for example, we've witnessed the migration of video into live streaming and platforms like TikTok and WhatsApp. At one time, video was understood as an alternative to the liveness of television. Now we have a completely different loop. It may seem like a very mundane infrastructure—used to share everything from press conferences to performance art to protests to mass murder—but live-streamed video still disrupts control systems, opening up all kinds of possibilities.

Machine interventions manage networks in ways we could never have imagined in the 1990s, but within these infrastructures we have all kinds of new mobilizations of people. In 2019, for example, there were widespread protests in India against a new citizenship law. A song based on a poem by the late Faiz Ahmed Faiz was widely shared and played at protests around the country; first set to music in the '80s, it has now been translated into more than sixteen languages. Dynamic live streaming, previously associated with Hindu nationalism, was also harnessed by protesters. Interventions are now scaled and distributed very rapidly: almost everyone has access to some form of video production and distribution, even if they're just forwarding content (fig. 8).

More than two decades ago, David Rodowick examined the shift away from models of cultural theory dominated by semiotics, which had privileged textual signification. Now confronted with computer-generated images, text was "losing its uniform contours, fixed spacing, and linear sense," he wrote. "It was impossible not be astonished by . . . how precisely space was 'textualized'; that is, how the Euclidian solidity of the image was fragmented, rendered discontinuous, divisible, and liable to recombination in the most precise ways." After the digital, "categories of thought are becoming increasingly nonlinear," as if marking the move from a regime of signs to an aesthetics of technologized sensation.[4] Now, after the COVID-19 pandemic, we may need a comparable move to come to terms with our significantly transformed sensory landscape. With the pandemic, video *became the world*, and it did so in ways that were vastly different from earlier decades. Video became a compressed archive of pandemic multiplicities, encompassing the mundane and the playful along with the irruptions of atmospheric terror that defined the pandemic experience.

The multiplication of space-times afforded by the smartphone and by app culture suggest that contemporary political aesthetics has folded stillness and motion into one another. In fact, those older oppositions make less and less sense today. The alternation between videos from temporary crowds and network-driven still images during recent protests in Sudan, India, and Iran are indicative of this new scenario. We know that networked infrastructures periodically create avenues for collective and micropolitical experiences. In this context, short videos mark time, fracture experiences, and produce remarkable networked experiences.

Paul Virilio believed that the potential for accidents is inherent in technological systems, as encapsulated in his idea of the integral accident. Large infrastructures try to minimize the potential for such crashes. Hacker networks, on the other hand, attach themselves to accelerating accidents. Today the accident continues to be important because there's an enduring threat of breakdown. What happens when internet cables are snapped? State-sponsored internet shutdowns, akin to the street curfews of the colonial era, can also prevent access. Since the Arab Spring, this has been the primary weapon of the state, designed to wall off contagious internet architectures and circulating video. In recent uprisings, protesters

4   David Rodowick, *Reading the Figural, or, Philosophy after the New Media* (Durham, NC: Duke University Press, 2001), 3, 108.

Fig. 9 Rabih Mroué. *The Pixelated Revolution*. 2012. Part I of the series The Fall of a Hair. High-definition video (color, sound), 22 min. The Museum of Modern Art, New York. Fund for the Twenty-First Century

5 Rabih Mroué, "The Pixelated Revolution," trans. Ziad Nawfal, *TDR/The Drama Review* 56, no. 3 (Fall 2012): 30.

seemed to fuse with their recording devices, suggesting what artist Rabih Mroué calls an "optical prosthesis"—as seen in his 2012 video *The Pixelated Revolution*, which investigates the role of smartphone cameras, social media, and texting during the recent Syrian Revolution (figs. 9, 10).[5] Prolonged internet shutdowns have been widely used in Xinjiang and Kashmir. In fact, while China has a sophisticated censorship firewall, India leads the world in internet shutdowns. Unsurprisingly, the colonial-era Section 144 of the Indian Penal Code, originally designed for crowd control, has been used to justify their legality.

How do we re-energize critique in the post-pandemic landscape, amid the hegemonic power of media-driven platform capitalism? Steven Shaviro has written that cameras are now machines for generating post-cinematic affect. The pandemic has drawn attention to the ways in which affect has been mobilized, calculated, and monetized. The technologies of attention and the modulation of affectivity that drive contemporary capitalism pose a challenge for the artistic traditions of negation and critique. In response, we have seen the emergence of the forensic turn, an approach pioneered by the multidisciplinary research group Forensic Architecture and manifested in a number of artist-driven projects included in *Signals*, such as Lawrence Abu Hamdan's *Walled Unwalled* (2018).

In their recent book *Investigative Aesthetics* (2021), Matthew Fuller and Eyal Weizman, founding director of Forensic Architecture, call for an anti-hegemonic strategy that addresses sensing and sense-making. This forensically driven aesthetics, they write, "is an approach that is

fundamentally about assembling, and finding the means to recognize, a multiplicity of different forms of sensation."[6] I'm interested in public interventions in which a broad range of actors are trying to unpack something that's seen as problematic or questionable. Open-source websites like Bellingcat have pioneered tools for investigating war atrocities by harvesting and verifying user videos. In India, Alt.news has emerged as a major resource for calling out regime disinformation and fake videos. This new forensics is an important intervention, one that speaks to our shifting conception of public life. It's an acknowledgment of the new stakes for media aesthetics today. In the twenty-first century, we've moved into a more challenging environment than that of the time when bodily perception was seen as extended by technological prosthesis, as Marshall McLuhan famously argued. Our post-pandemic sensory world is deeply pharmacological: toxic and curative, exciting and dangerous, a place where endless media saturation forces us to revisit ideas of life itself.

As told to Rattanamol Singh Johal and Michelle Kuo

Fig. 10 Rabih Mroué. *The Pixelated Revolution.* 2012

Opposite CAMP. *From Gulf to Gulf to Gulf.* 2013

6 Matthew Fuller and Eyal Weizman, *Investigative Aesthetics: Conflict and Commons in the Politics of Truth* (London: Verso, 2021), 35.

Victor Masayesva Jr.
(Native American, born 1951)

RITUAL CLOWNS. 1988
Standard-definition video
(color, sound), 18 min.

Since the 1980s, Victor Masayesva Jr. has demonstrated the ways in which video and computer technologies can uphold—or undermine—Native and Indigenous communities' control of their histories. In *Ritual Clowns*, he deftly alters anthropological footage of Hopi dancers using montage, voice-over, and animation to explore the educational and cleansing role of clowns in Southwest Pueblo plaza traditions across generations. Made using the supercomputers at Broadway Video—the New York entertainment and media company known for producing *Saturday Night Live*—Masayesva's freewheeling animations guide the viewer through the work, which includes depictions of land and children in costume as well as traditional dancing and storytelling.

In his essay "Indigenous Experimentalism," Masayesva writes, "Experimental films and videos can be defined by the degree to which they subvert the colonizers' indoctrination and champion indigenous expression in the political landscape." True to his words, in *Ritual Clowns* Masayesva both asserts Indigenous authorship of Hopi history and disrupts the colonizing gaze of the anthropological footage, material long used to produce and reinforce stereotypical depictions of native peoples. The artist distributed *Ritual Clowns* in the 1980s but then removed the work from circulation to reconsider the privacy of the cultural knowledge it depicts. In recent years, he has exhibited it on a case-by-case basis. Reinforcing Masayesva's experimental vision, this distribution history offers further evidence of the active role video can play in affirming Indigenous sovereignty.

LILIA ROCIO TABOADA

Mona Hatoum
(British-Palestinian, born 1952)

MEASURES OF DISTANCE. 1988
Standard-definition video
(color, sound), 15:26 min.

"My dear Mona, the apple of my eyes, how I miss you and long to feast my eyes on your beautiful face that brightens up my days." Thus begins a voice-over delivered by the artist, reading an English translation of a letter she received in London from her mother in Beirut. Translated segments of their correspondence alternate with snippets of conversation between the two women in Levantine Arabic. The video's visuals, meanwhile, move through composite images Hatoum constructed by layering the letters' handwritten Arabic text with stills of her mother in the shower. Offering an intimate portrait of a mother-daughter relationship across a geographical and generational divide, the work asks how familial bonds can be maintained amid displacement and exile necessitated by occupation and war. The artist plays with perception—tweaking scale, material, language, and narrative conventions—to disorient viewers and disrupt easy legibility.

Hatoum was born in Beirut to displaced Palestinian parents and ultimately settled in London, where she was stranded on a visit as civil war broke out in Lebanon. Her performance and video works from the 1980s refer to this history, experimenting with form and media to evoke visceral feelings of longing and the alienation that pervades the diasporic condition. Hatoum's works in this period can be situated alongside those of her postcolonial peers and predecessors in England, an affiliation signaled by her inclusion in the landmark touring show *The Other Story: Afro-Asian Artists in Post-War Britain*, organized by artist and curator Rasheed Araeen for London's Hayward Gallery in 1989. These works share certain formal and conceptual strategies: deliberate concealment, layering, gaps, slippages, and untranslatable language. *Measures of Distance* was, in Hatoum's words, "constructed visually in such a way that every frame speaks of literal closeness and implied distance."

RATTANAMOL SINGH JOHAL

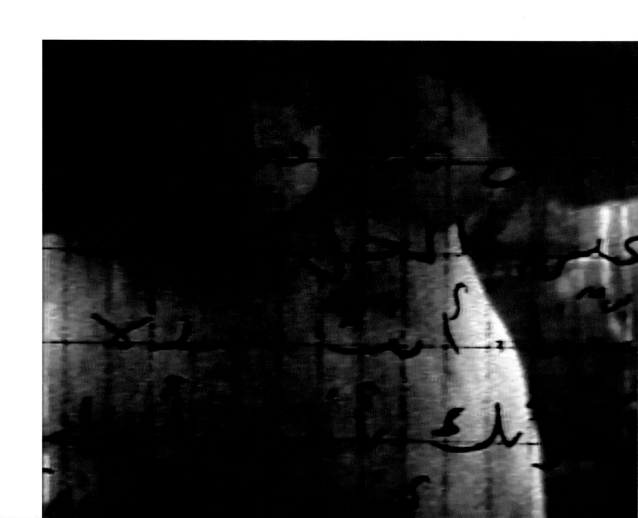

Gretchen Bender
(American, 1951–2004)

TV TEXT AND IMAGE (DONNELL LIBRARY CENTER VERSION). 1990
Live television broadcast on twelve cathode-ray-tube monitors, vinyl lettering, and shelves, dimensions variable

Gretchen Bender conceived this iteration of her series TV Text and Image (1986–91) for the front window of the New York Public Library's Donnell Library Center, which was situated directly across the street from The Museum of Modern Art in midtown Manhattan. First installed in January 1990, the work comprises twelve television sets, each tuned to a different channel and each featuring a phrase—such as "Narcotics of Surrealism," "Military Research," or "Homeless"—lettered in vinyl on its screen. The texts are superimposed over the otherwise unmediated flow of programming, prompting a critical engagement with the electronic images coursing beneath them. The work is, by definition, continually updated, and today the "channels" may include digital streaming networks or internet TV rather than traditional broadcast or cable. But now, as then, an endless flow of grotesquely flattened scenes of violence and desire—in sitcoms, commercials, news, dramas, war footage, product placements, and reality TV—is seen through a scrim of words that seem to spell out television's unspoken referents: the conditions of poverty and authoritarianism that normally lie beneath its glossy spectacles.

Like many of her peers in the 1980s, Bender incorporated images from popular culture into artworks that offered a critique of the contemporary mediascape. She was among the earliest to bring these appropriation tactics to television, which was, she noted, "an incredible goldmine for the flow of the pulse, the permutations that happen daily, in the culture." She continued, "I'll mimic the media—but I'll turn up the voltage on the currents so high that hopefully it will blast criticality out there."

LINA KAVALIUNAS

Right Installation view, Donnell Library Center, West Fifty-Third Street, New York, January 1990

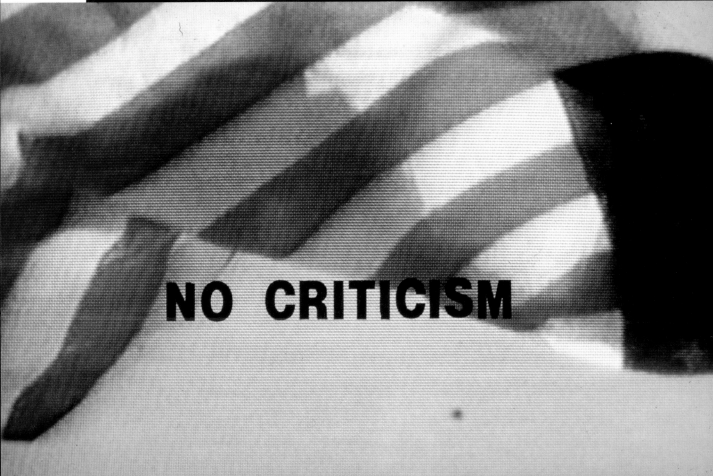

MILITARY RESEARCH

PEOPLE WITH AIDS

COMMUNITY
bulletin board
HOMELESS
Mer ...... Hall
At Abraham Goodman
House, Hosting Feb
Events, Call For Listings
Info 362 8060

CIVIL RIGHTS

NO CRITICISM

Left Artist's composite of stills from the TV Text and Image series, 1986–91

Opposite Details from the TV Text and Image series, 1986–91

SELF-CENSORSHIP

MUSCLE BEACH VENICE

BODY OWNERSHIP

Marlon Riggs
(American, 1957–1994)

ANTHEM. 1991
Standard-definition video (black
and white and color, sound), 9 min.

Anthem begins with a cut and mix of language and images: a butch queen in yellow sunglasses and headscarf; two buff, shirtless men kissing; a cock ring; a rose; and a billowing American flag. Excerpts from poems by Essex Hemphill and Colin Robinson, among others, are recited over this montage, accompanied by a pumping house-music score. While appropriating the quick cuts and other visual tropes of MTV music videos, *Anthem* perverts the genre by highlighting Black queer intersectionality. For example, in one scene the red, black, and green color scheme of Marcus Garvey's pan-African flag appears within an outline of the continent of Africa, which is overlaid with an image of the pink triangle from ACT UP's Silence=Death poster, a mash-up of Black nationalism and AIDS activism that refuses a binary separation between the two. Although *Anthem* features Marlon Riggs prominently, dancing with abandon in garments ranging from leather gear to a patterned frock to a kente-cloth kufi, the filmmaker, poet, and activist called on many others to recite and sing and perform as well, as if to embody the declaration (borrowed from the poet Langston Hughes) that closes the video: "I, too, sing America." The result is a vital anthology of and testament to Black cultural production in the early 1990s.

GLENN LIGON

131

Song Dong
(Chinese, born 1966)

BROKEN MIRROR. 1999
Standard-definition video
(color, sound), 3:54 min.

In this single-channel video, the artist has recorded himself shattering a mirror at twelve different locations in Beijing—from crowded transit hubs to quiet plazas to the historic Tiananmen Square. In each scene, shot from ground level, he holds a mirror up to the portable video camera, allowing it to surreptitiously witness and record views of everyday life behind or at an oblique angle to him. Then, using the hammer he holds in his other hand, he swiftly breaks the pane, shattering the seamless reflection and revealing the scene behind it. His camera also captures the startled expressions, cocked heads, and gasps of curious passersby, who soon resume their banal routines.

Throughout his long career, Song has used video to evoke both the potential of the individual to intervene in sociopolitical conditions and the probable futility of those efforts. Like the reflection in a mirror, the images of reality generated by a video camera carry with them a presumption of accuracy and transparency. Song's ephemeral public interventions in *Broken Mirror* quite literally smash this impression of truthfulness, suggesting that video technology might easily be put to insidious and invasive uses. Perhaps alluding to this disillusionment, in the final destructive act of *Broken Mirror* he bares his face to the mirror before breaking it to expose a desolate and silent passageway beyond.

WONG BINGHAO

Walid Raad
(Lebanese, born 1967)
Souheil Bachar

HOSTAGE: THE BACHAR TAPES (ENGLISH VERSION). 2001
Standard-definition video (color, sound), 16:17 min.

Hostage: The Bachar Tapes (English Version) draws on the artist's doctoral research into the images and texts surrounding the widely reported kidnappings of Western men in Lebanon in the 1980s and early '90s. The video presents a fragmented first-person account by Souheil Bachar, an Arab man who was, we are told, held in the same cell as five well-documented Euro-American hostages for twenty-seven weeks in 1985. Introductory titles state that Bachar is the producer and narrator of fifty-three videotapes recounting his time in captivity. Of these, he has authorized only two for screening in Western Europe and North America, translated and dubbed, he specifies, in "a neutral-toned female voice." Clips from the extensive television coverage of the kidnappings are interleaved with Bachar's story, which includes an account of sexual activity among the prisoners, revealing aspects of the power dynamics in the cell and underscoring the fetishization and fear of Arab men. Bachar also discusses the multiple memoirs published by the white hostages, catalyzing a reflection on the subjectivities, visibility, and relative expressive agency of the countless Arabs who suffered through the devastating conflicts of the 1970s, '80s, and '90s. Both the promise and the problem of access to these experiences are signaled in the work by the conceit of a limited release, the contrived nature of the media splicing, the visual abstractions and sonic disturbances in the tape, and the narrative non sequiturs and significant misalignments (imperceptible to non-Arabic speakers) between Bachar's spoken account and the translated narration.

Hostage is a key example of Raad's parafictional treatment of the Lebanese Civil War. The artist weaves together verifiable historical episodes and entities with elaborately concocted characters and other fictions in a manner that appears credible while subtly revealing flaws, fabrications, and the limits of representation. The work is included in the archives of The Atlas Group, the overarching entity Raad created for research, documentation, and speculation on the history of Lebanon during the war. It was shown in Documenta 11, the 2002 edition of the international art exhibition, organized by Okwui Enwezor, which has come to represent a paradigm shift in the discussion and display of global video- and documentary-based practices.

RATTANAMOL SINGH JOHAL

Artur Żmijewski
(Polish, born 1966)

DEMOCRACIES. 2009
Twenty-channel high-definition video (color, sound), 146 min.

Between 2007 and 2009, Artur Żmijewski and a team of five videographers recorded a series of public assemblies. Immersing themselves in crowds in countries across Europe and the Middle East, the camera crew captured the sights and sounds of bodies congregating, communicating, and occupying public space. The straightforward, minimal footage that resulted was then edited into the twenty videos comprising *Democracies*. The work's multiple channels play simultaneously, their audio tracks mixing into an ever-shifting soundscape of political passion and even mass hysteria. Shouts, songs, horns, and shots ring out from every direction, their origins nearly impossible to discern.

The videos present different political motivations and collective demands, a variety of voices, movements, and guises. In one, Palestinians gathered in the West Bank for a protest against Israeli occupation are greeted with rubber bullets. In another, mourners somberly watch as soldiers march the rose-covered casket of a far-right Austrian politician across a public square. Violence erupts during anti-NATO demonstrations in France; raucous German and Turkish football fans watch a championship match on an outdoor video screen; Polish union members at a demonstration proclaim their desire to "live with dignity." Similarities emerge throughout disparate scenes: we witness bodies exercising a right to appear, to lay claim to public space. We also see the state's policing and delimiting of public space, in the form of riot police and tear gas or as metal barriers designating where and how people may stand in city streets.

In a 2009 interview, Żmijewski revealed that he "chose the title *Democracies* because it's a lie: these are not all democracies." Or, rather, they may be democratic nations, but within and beyond their borders they engage in practices that undercut or threaten the democracy they claim to uphold. The mass confronts this threat. Bodies assemble in the street and together demand a different future.

LINA KAVALIUNAS

Amar Kanwar
(Indian, born 1964)

THE TORN FIRST PAGES. 2004–08
Nineteen-channel standard-definition video (black and white and color, sound and silent; varying durations), nineteen sheets of paper, three metal frames, books, magazines, and artist books, dimensions variable

This three-part, nineteen-channel video installation considers questions of time, memory, and evidence as they relate to Myanmar's decades-old pro-democracy movement. Its title alludes to a poetic gesture of protest by Ko Than Htay, a Mandalay-based bookseller, against the country's Burmese military dictatorship. Than Htay tore the first page out of each book and journal he sold in his shop—the page that, as mandated by law, featured declarations of the government's political, economic, and social objectives. For this action, he was arrested in December 1994 and subjected to three years of imprisonment and torture.

Referring both to the torn leaves of Than Htay's books and an accumulation of evidence documenting the regime's atrocities, Kanwar's installation presents a selection of printed materials as well as a series of short videos. The moving-image vignettes, projected onto sheets of paper suspended from three metal armatures in a darkened gallery, were produced using footage shot by activists—often at great personal risk—and dispersed through local and diasporic networks via the internet or computer disks. *The Face* (2004) is based on an unauthorized recording of a visit by Senior General Than Shwe to the site of Mahatma Gandhi's cremation in New Delhi. Kanwar uses slow motion, zoom, rewind, and replay to underscore the absurdity of the encounter, in which the military dictator threw pink rose petals onto the memorial then repeated the gesture at the urging of official photographers. *Ma Win Maw Oo* (2005) focuses on a grainy news image of the limp body of the eponymous high-school student, carried by two medical trainees after she was shot dead during the 1988 uprising against the regime. Other accounts of violence, exile, and dissent call attention to the present, documenting the continuing resilience of political protest worldwide as well as the persistent brutality of authoritarian regimes, including the one in Myanmar, where a supposed transition to democracy in 2011 has been followed by ongoing genocidal killings of the minority Muslim Rohingya population.

RATTANAMOL SINGH JOHAL

Right Installation view, Haus der Kunst, Munich, 2008
Opposite, top Still from *The Face* (2004), from Part I of *The Torn First Pages*
Opposite, bottom Installation view (detail), Marian Goodman Gallery, New York, 2010

Top and bottom Stills from *Somewhere in May* (2005), from Part I of *The Torn First Pages*

Carlos Motta
(Colombian, born 1978)

WE WHO FEEL DIFFERENTLY. 2012
Custom platforms and seating, carpet, 5-channel high-definition video (color, sound; varying durations), 5 custom LCD monitors, desktop computer, website, 6 sets of headphones, inkjet print mounted on wood, 4 inkjet prints on paper, and vinyl lettering, dimensions variable

We Who Feel Differently explores dissident perspectives on queer activism from the 1960s to 2012. The documentary video installation includes fifty interviews conducted by Carlos Motta with activists, academics, and artists in Colombia, the United States, Norway, and South Korea. Disheartened by the turn in the Global North toward a rights-based framework for LGBTIQQ activism, Motta uses the conversations to consider the political positions made possible when difference is centered instead of equality. Noting that lesbian, gay, bisexual, trans, intersex, queer, and questioning people "have learned to assimilate and to conform to those very things that [their] predecessors . . . fought against," the artist argues that their increasing inclusion within state institutions like marriage and the military should not be recognized as progress. The work's five video monitors materialize the multiple perspectives that are a necessary condition for democratic discourse. Motta designed the installation with architect Daniel Greenfield as a "social sculpture that allows Museum visitors . . . to gather and interact amongst themselves," he has said. "The use of colors, the design of pattern, and the distribution of the elements refer to the graphic emblems of the sexual liberation movement." Maximizing accessibility, the work also exists as a website (wewhofeeldifferently.info) with multilingual transcripts of the interviews, a PDF of the book Motta produced based on them, and a digital journal with new writing on LGBTIQQ politics.

BRANDON ENG

It reflects the desire to control everything outside governmental supervision.

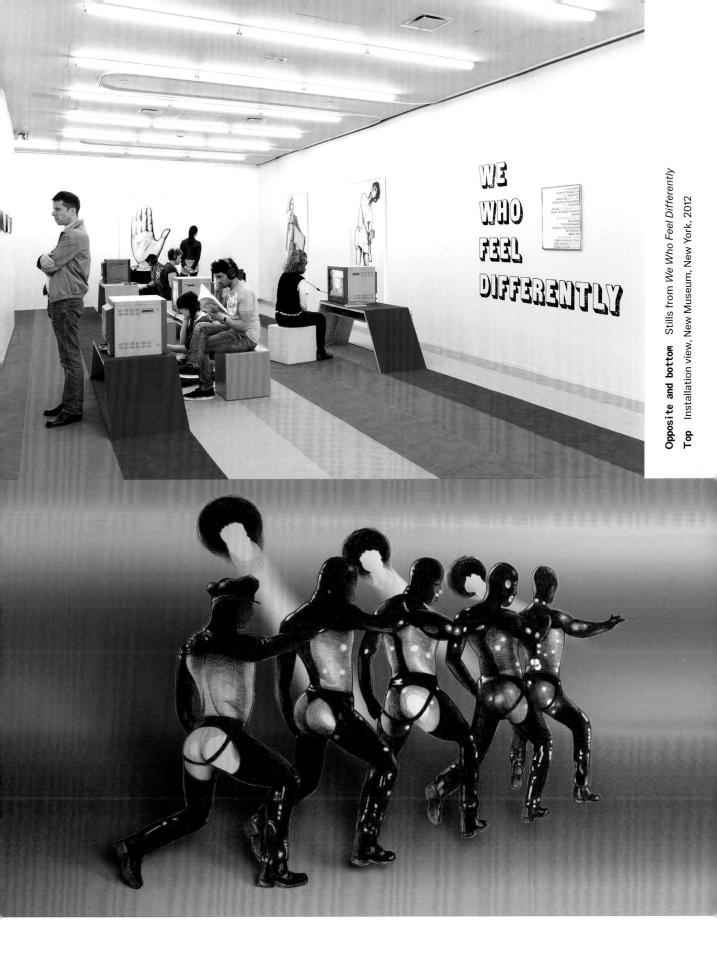

WE WHO FEEL DIFFERENTLY

Opposite and bottom Stills from *We Who Feel Differently*

Top Installation view, New Museum, New York, 2012

I don't know how much it will contribute to
people being more tolerant or less violent,

but it does generate transformations and, at least, it brings a political project to light.

Sondra Perry
(American, born 1986)

DOUBLE QUADRUPLE ETCETERA ETCETERA I & II. 2013
Two-channel high-definition video (color, silent), 9 min.

In *Double Quadruple Etcetera Etcetera I & II*, the dancers Danny Giles and Joiri Minaya perform in the artist's studio. As they move energetically across the space, the white walls appear to take over their bodies, an effect achieved through software that uses artificial intelligence to replace an object—or face, or body—in a digital image with content sampled from other parts of the picture. As such, the work typifies the artist's practice of using postproduction editing tools to examine the ways Black people may shapeshift and self-create in digital spaces. "The preoccupations of my work are around technologies of representation, technologies of lenses, surveillance," she has said, "how Blackness or Black culture show up in those spaces, how they navigate, how they explode representation altogether."

Perry considers digital space to be a place of possibility and fluidity. Here she demonstrates that it may also be a site of erasure, as the performers are consumed by the picture's background. At the same time, despite the efforts of the software, their bodies repeatedly flash into visibility, and the frenetic whiplash of their hair is constantly visible, beyond the control of the all-seeing computer eye. The possibility of assimilation is acknowledged, but it is clear that it might never be fully achieved. Even in digital spaces, the body may be a tool of refusal.

MARIELLE INGRAM

Chto Delat
(Russia, founded 2003)

THE EXCLUDED. IN
A MOMENT OF DANGER. 2014
Four-channel high-definition
video (color, sound), 56:46 min.

What is to be done? The question is an open-ended yet urgent call to action. In Saint Petersburg, in 2003, a band of artists, philosophers, and writers took this query, in Russian, as their name: *Chto delat?* The collective drew its appellation from the 1863 novel by dissident writer Nikolai Chernyshevsky, calling it a "sort of manual on how to construct emancipatory collectives and make them sustainable within a hostile society." Chernyshevsky had written and published the text while imprisoned, awaiting trial on charges of radicalism. He was sent to Siberia in 1864, but his book's political influence could not be contained: it inspired thousands, including Lenin, who penned his own *Chto delat?* in 1902.

A decade into Chernyshevsky's exile, the publisher Ippolit Myshkin tried and failed to rescue the captive. Myshkin, who had been on the run following a state raid of his small political press, was then imprisoned himself. Refusing to succumb to government pressure, he delivered impassioned speeches and struggled for freedom until his execution in 1885. In 2014, as the Russian government's annexation of Crimea plunged the country into a new and brutal political situation, this largely forgotten figure became a touchstone for Chto Delat, inspiring this four-channel, twelve-episode work.

Unlike video installations that assemble and appropriate gathered footage or use live feeds, *The Excluded. In a Moment of Danger* deliberately employs the strategies of what critic Maria Lind has called "theatrical documentary." Drawing specifically on modes of political theater, the video features graduates from the group's School of Engaged Art gesturing and vocalizing as they perform responses to the intertitles that precede each episode. In the first, "the film participants log onto social networks." Gazes locked on screens, they scroll through images of protest and war, the sound of clicking keys radiating from their laptops. The fourth episode shows participants realizing "that they are a part of society and responsible for it." They stare directly at the viewer, their bodies moving more and more spasmodically until they collapse on the floor. Episode ten has the participants commemorating "unlucky heroes in history": Myshkin is invoked, as are internet activist Aaron Swartz and the Russian protesters detained in 2012 for demonstrating against Putin's third inauguration. "Any one of us could be in their place," one woman intones. As they speak, the participants gradually form a pile with their bodies, a makeshift monument to their heroes.

"What can be done with this state of affairs?" Chto Delat asks in a short text accompanying the work. "We lost. But we are prepared to learn from our mistakes. Where were our mistakes? What were they? Where did we go wrong?" *The Excluded. In a Moment of Danger* takes up these questions, searching for "pathways to transform our weakness into strength, our defeat into victory." By examining our failures, the group suggests, we may discover a way to forge ahead.

LINA KAVALIUNAS

Top Installation view, *Time Capsule. Artistic Report on Catastrophes and Utopia*, Secession, Vienna, 2014

Bottom and following pages Stills from *The Excluded. In a Moment of Danger*

I was born in the year
that the USSR collapsed.

Ming Wong
(Singaporean, born 1971)

WINDOWS ON THE WORLD (PART 2). 2014
24-channel standard-definition video (color, sound; varying durations), 24 flat-screen monitors, MDF, wood, and steel, overall (approx.): 65″ × 13′ 1 ½″ × 30″ (165 × 400 × 75 cm)

In *Windows on the World (Part 2)*, twenty-four video channels display scenes of space travel and extraterrestrial colonization gathered by the artist from various post–Cultural Revolution Chinese media sources. The work's monitors are installed in a concave metal structure that conjures the control station of a futuristic spacecraft. Science-fiction films, television shows, and animations appear alongside actual news broadcasts that chronicle Chinese activities in space. Offering a compendium of ways in which Chinese cultural production has imagined a future for the communist government—and its citizens—beyond Earth, the work captures how, along with a shared sense of history, a collective vision of the future helps to structure national identity and a sense of progress. By cataloging a selection of nationalistic futures, Wong's work reveals the contributions of broadcast television and film distribution networks to the top-down dissemination of cultural identity.

The assemblage is set to a soundtrack that combines sci-fi sound effects with Cantonese opera, one of China's oldest operatic forms. Its popularity in Hong Kong has allowed it to thrive relatively free from state intervention, while in mainland China it has been refined to reflect values associated with the People's Republic of China. The work's sonic environment reminds us that cultural production always encodes specific ideologies, regardless of the technology enabling it.

Windows on the World (Part 2) is an important hinge between twentieth- and twenty-first-century forms of media distribution. The work's footage was originally disseminated in cinemas and TV broadcasts, and yet here Wong has assembled it into a kind of database, a system whose omnipresence grows ever more pronounced in the new millennium. Unlike broadcasts, which transmit content once and in one direction to a large population, databases make media perpetually available and accessible, even interactive—qualities Ming exploits to create new meaning out of an accumulation of content.

GIAMPAOLO BIANCONI

Opposite Installation view, *Social Factory: The 10th Shanghai Biennale*, 2014

Top Still from *Windows on the World (Part 2)*

Bottom Composite of stills from *Windows on the World (Part 2)*

RADIO
CCTV 13
直播
手持摄像机拍摄图像
20世纪初，科幻小说首次由晚清改革者、学者、记者、哲学家梁启超，以及中国现代文学之父鲁迅，以翻译西方作品的形式传入中国。
他们相信科幻作品能在中国传播先进知识，并且能推动这个落后于西方工业化国家的民族发展。
Science fiction first appeared in China through translations of Western authors at the beginning of the 20th century by Liang Qichao, the scholar, journalist, philosopher and reformist of late Qing and early Republican China; and Lu Xun,_
LIVE
ASTRONAUT EXITS ORBITAL MODULE
珊瑚岛上的
死光

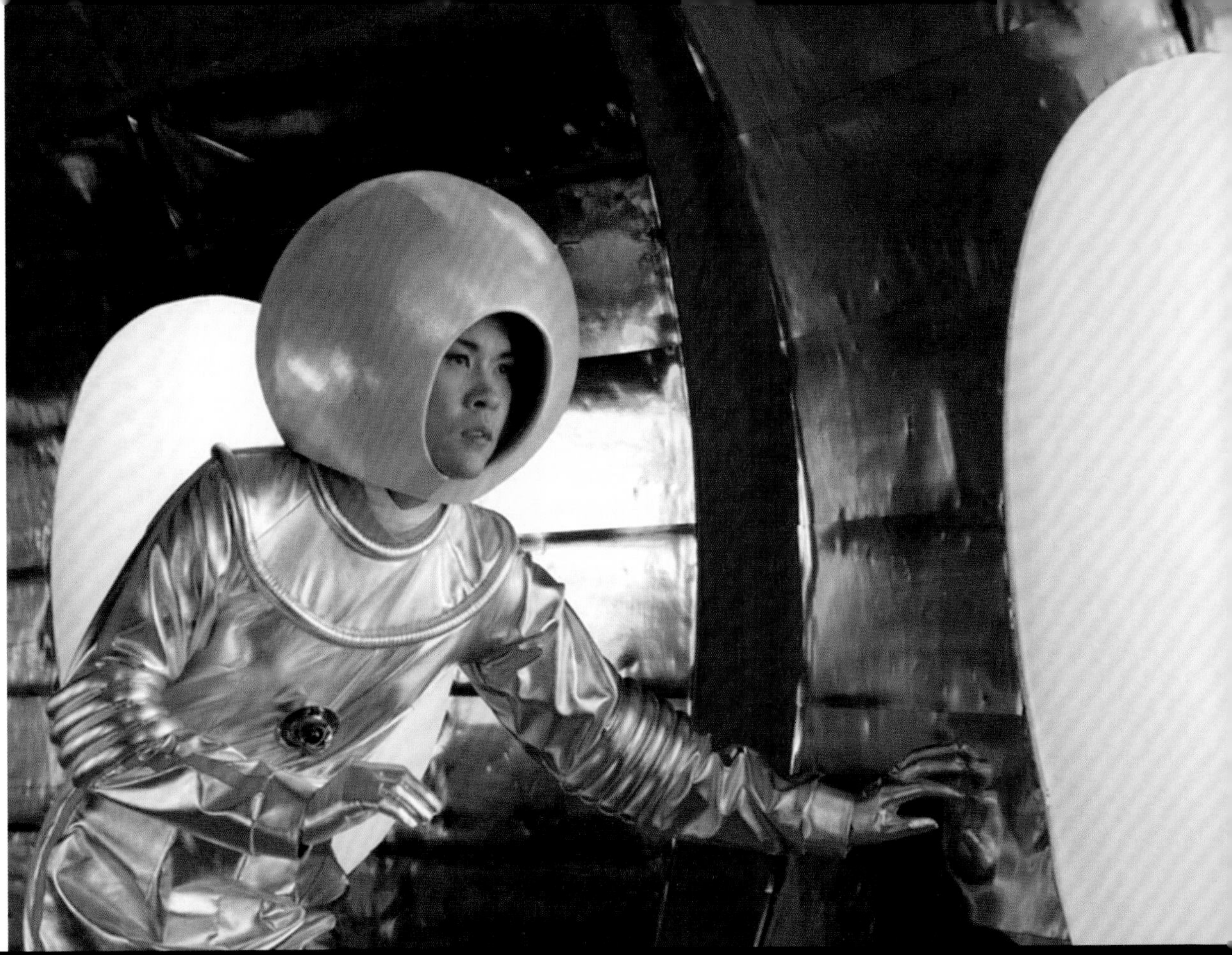

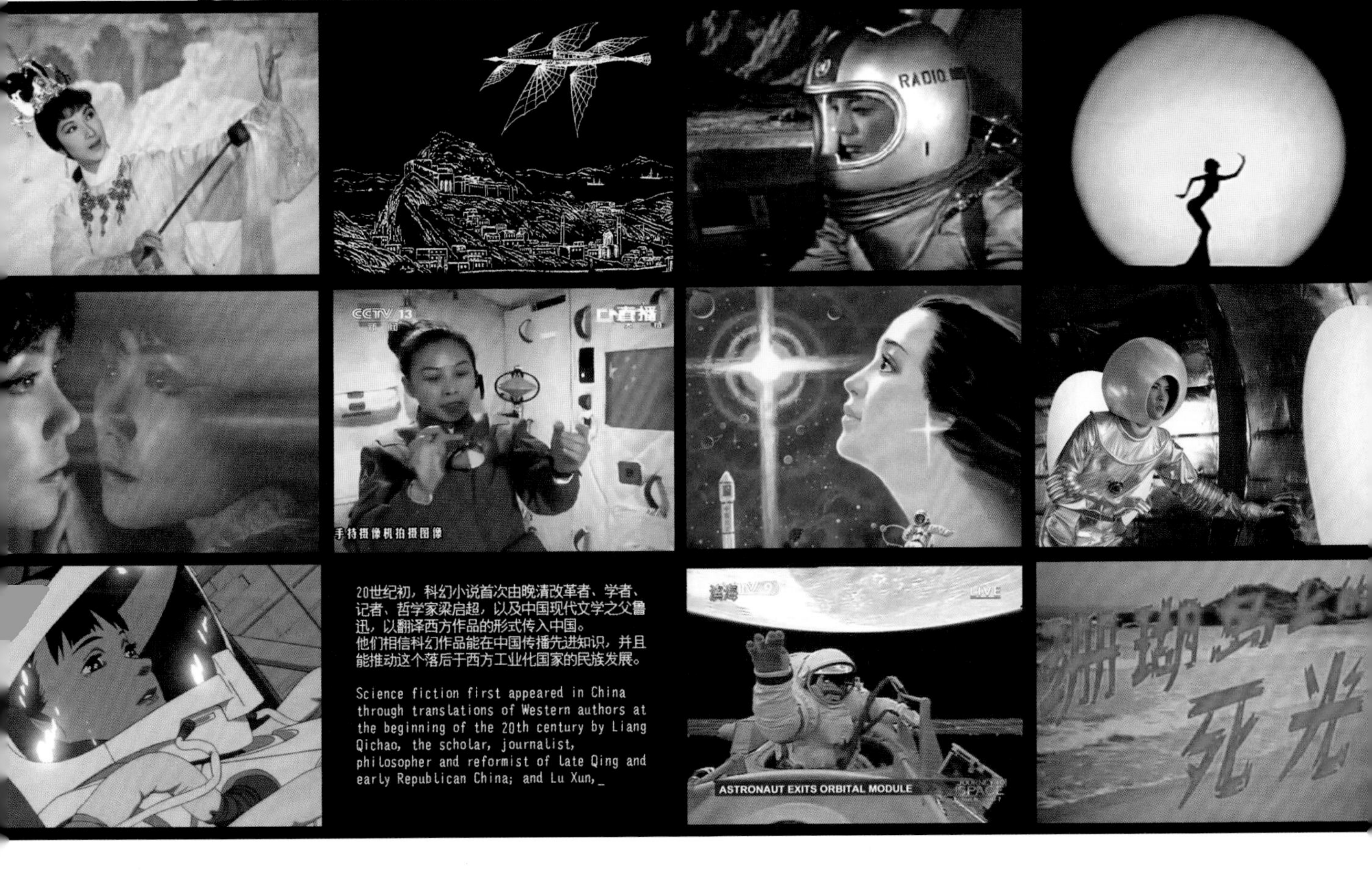

Martine Syms
(American, born 1988)

Nobody ever told me that I was an African woman.

Nobody ever told me what the history of African people was.

*Nobody ever told me that America is business and
without business you will have nothing and be nothing.*

*And nobody ever told me how to organize so that
I could develop institutions in my own community.*

*Now the sincerity of all programs and of all education
must be questioned, indicted, and convicted…*

These words are spoken in *Lessons I–CLXXX* by Sister Souljah—
an impassioned social activist, emcee, and novelist—on a 1990s
TV talk show, telling a primarily white audience about the injus-
tices associated with race and class in America. Her story is one
of many in Martine Syms's work, an extended visual poem comprising 180 video shorts, each thirty seconds long. Structured
as cantos—the foundational segments of epic poetry—*Lessons*
nods to poet Kevin Young's seminal anthology *The Grey Album:
On the Blackness of Blackness* (2012), which investigates
a tradition of improvisation and storytelling in Black American
culture while simultaneously arguing that Black American culture *is* American culture.

LESSONS I–CLXXX. 2014–18
180 standard- and high-definition videos (color, sound), 90 min. (30 sec. each)

Syms considers each thirty-second segment as a kind
of advertisement or commercial that sifts through everyday
events, art, music, and popular culture to foreground a lesson
or core tenet of the Black radical tradition. Consisting of found
footage, including homemade videos, clips from talk shows
and popular sitcoms, memes, and YouTube content, the work
parses a stunning variety of visual languages to make pal-
pable the aesthetics and politics of identity. Produced over
a span of four years, *Lessons* uses the computer-programming
language Max to randomize the internal order of the segments.
This refusal to engage in linear narration reflects an aesthetic
method deployed by many Black radicals in their work. By alter-
ing traditional narrative, Syms creates an ever-shifting and
complex cultural history, one that is subject to systems of control but also uses spontaneity and lore to amplify reality.

DANIELLE A. JACKSON

ME
LOOKING
LOOKING

Opposite and previous pages Stills from *Lessons I–CLXXX*

Top Installation view, Storage by Hyundai Card, Seoul, 2022, with the wall painting *GIRRRLGIRLLLGGGIRLGIIIRL* (2017)

Bottom Installation view, Art Basel, 2018

Lawrence Abu Hamdan

WALLED UNWALLED. 2018
High-definition video
(color, sound), 20:04 min.

Much of Lawrence Abu Hamdan's work is based on knowledge gleaned from sound. Mimicking the surveillance apparatuses of the modern state, the artist collects, processes, and interprets acoustic data related to crimes and human rights violations using sophisticated technological tools and research methods developed with the London-based research group Forensic Architecture. The resulting "earwitness testimony" is a form of forensic evidence that may be presented in international tribunals or courts of law.

Walled Unwalled is based on an extended period of investigative activity, tracking legal cases and historical events in which the passage of sound through walls was a crucial factor. These include the 2014 trial of the South African sprinter Oscar Pistorius, who shot his girlfriend Reeva Steenkamp four times through a locked door, as well as acts of torture perpetrated at the infamous Saydnaya military prison in Syria. In the latter case, former prisoners, who had been held in windowless cells and often blindfolded, were asked to recollect what they had heard in confinement, allowing Abu Hamdan (and his collaborators from Forensic Architecture and Amnesty International) to reconstruct modes of torture and the spatial layout of the prison. In *Walled Unwalled*, the artist presents these narratives in a twenty-minute performance-lecture, recorded in the sound-effects studios at Funkhaus Berlin, a Cold War–era radio broadcasting facility located in the former GDR. The resulting video is projected onto a screen that is viewed through a transparent glass wall, architecturally invoking the conceptual paradox at the work's core—namely, that walls are forces of both containment and transmission.

Walls are still built to block visual and physical access, but new scientific discoveries have made them increasingly permeable: states and other actors are developing and deploying military-grade technologies to "see" through solid structures, thereby extending their information-gathering capabilities and domains of control. "Now, no wall on earth is impermeable," Abu Hamdan has declared. "Today, we're all wall and no wall at all."

RATTANAMOL SINGH JOHAL

Top Still from *Walled Unwalled*

Bottom Installation view, *The Sound of Screens Imploding*, Biennale de l'Image en Mouvement, Centre d'Art Contemporain Genève, 2018

Top Still from *Walled Unwalled*

Bottom Installation view, *Natq*, Sfeir-Semler Gallery, Beirut, 2019

Top Still from *Walled Unwalled*

Bottom Installation view, *The Sound of Screens Imploding*, Biennale de l'Image en Mouvement, Centre d'Art Contemporain Genève, 2018

165

Dana Kavelina
(Ukrainian, born 1995)

LETTER TO A TURTLEDOVE. 2020
High-definition video
(color, sound), 20:55 min.

Letter to a Turtledove is a dreamlike video-poem that brings together archival footage and amateur video and interweaves them with spoken word, animation, and newly filmed scenes by the artist. The central source is the anonymous five-hour documentary *To Watch the War* (2018), a compilation of found video from the ongoing war in the Donbas, in eastern Ukraine. Reappropriating some of this material, Kavelina combined it with archival footage of the region, which was a key site of industrialization under Stalin in the 1930s. Donetsk, the largest city in the Donbas, was a mining town and later the Soviet "City of a Million Roses," a transformation that encapsulated a multitude of traumas, horrors, and hopes.

Initially, Kavelina conceived her film as a radio play. "The word 'letter,' in this case, actually refers to a radio signal, or call, addressed to a woman in the occupied territories—a message intercepted by someone on the other side of the front line," she has said. The narration makes analogies between the land and a woman's body: "There is love between missile and earth.

A missile makes love to the earth, to stone and rebar. . . . Coal mines are born of this love, and dead bodies, which you gather up and plant in your garden." Through visual collage, poetry, and constant interruption, *Letter to a Turtledove* transmits a fiercely alternative depiction of the war from a woman's perspective—pointing to the fact that rape and femicide are a constant yet often unarticulated consequence of military conflict.

INGA LĀCE

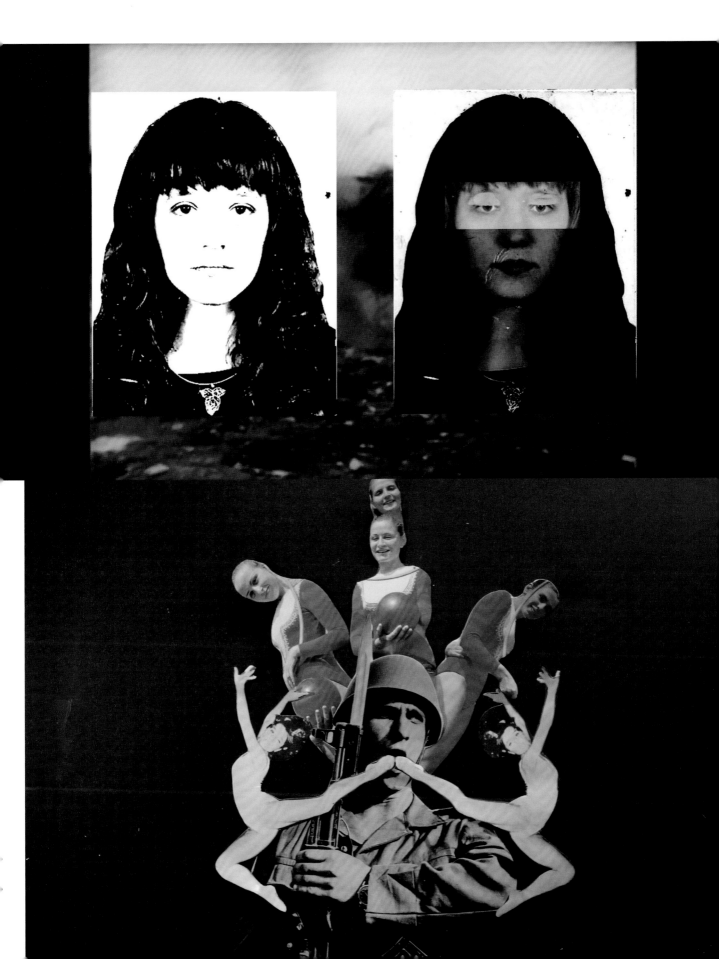

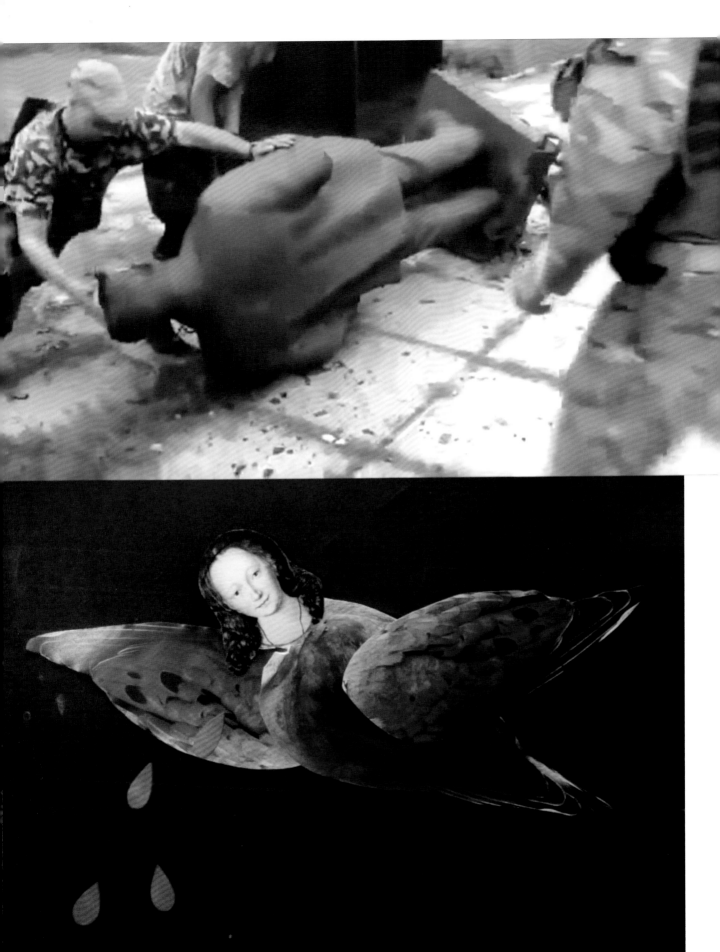

Sandra Mujinga
(Norwegian, born Congo 1989)

PERVASIVE LIGHT. 2021
Three-channel high-definition video (color, sound; 16:15 min.) and three flat-screen monitors, dimensions variable. Performed by Mariama Ndure

In Sandra Mujinga's *Pervasive Light*, an ethereal figure played by the Norwegian musician Mariama Ndure appears to move within and between three vertical monitors. Shrouded in a luminous cloak made by the artist from fabric that disappears against a green-screen backdrop, Ndure appears to mystify the camera's gaze, hovering between absence and presence. Accompanied by an undulating electronic soundtrack, she performs a series of gestures—hovering, pacing, removing her hood—but flickers out of view just as quickly as she appears.

Mujinga's triptych is a volatile portrait from a place and time we cannot locate. The work is shown in an unlit gallery; darkness envelops the viewer, creating a feeling of isolation from the outside world. By turns doubled, tripled, or swallowed whole, Ndure vanishes and emerges as she chooses, casting a spectral glow of liquid, oversaturated colors. Freeing her protagonist from conventional modes of image making and representation, Mujinga has created a choreography of resistance—and a meditation on the conditional visibility of Blackness in the mass media and in today's surveillance culture.

Pervasive Light is emblematic of Mujinga's wide-ranging practice, which encompasses video, installation, sculpture, textiles, and music. Drawing from video-game technology, science fiction, colonial history, and Afrofuturism, the artist contemplates the ways in which the digital realm fails to capture the expansiveness of lived experience and yet enables ways of being we never knew existed.

ERICA PAPERNIK-SHIMIZU

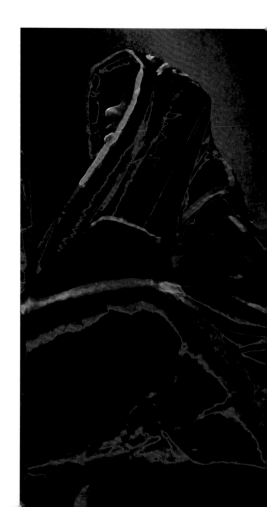

171

First television broadcast via the Telstar satellite, 1962

A Short History of Video Technology and Transmission

From the first television broadcast in Cuba to the launch of streaming video, this timeline lists just a few of the many twists and turns in the development of video and communication technologies over the past 125 years, tracing the birth and evolution of the devices, standards, and methods of transmission that have, for better or worse, shaped our world.

1897 First cathode-ray tube developed. Theorizing the device's potential, German physicist Karl Ferdinand Braun describes how its flow of electrons might one day be used to draw images on a screen.

1901 Amid a flurry of experimentation with wireless technology in Western nations, a Morse code message sent from Cornwall, England, is received in St. John's, Newfoundland—the first successful radio transmission across the Atlantic.

1906 The development of the Audion vacuum tube—an electronic amplifier—makes broadcast radio transmission possible. The technology begins to expand globally throughout the 1910s and '20s.

1911 Using a cathode-ray-tube device, Russian engineers Vladimir Zworykin and Boris Rosing transmit an image of four luminous bands.

1922 American Telephone and Telegraph Company (AT&T) launches WEAF, a "for hire" commercial radio station in New York, establishing the US system of funding broadcasting through the sale of "tolls" or advertisements.

1923 Zworykin, now based in the United States, applies for a patent for an electronic television system that synthesizes Russian innovations in television systems and the German cathode-ray-tube display. This leads to his development, in 1931, of the iconoscope, an image-capture tube that is the foundational element of the video camera.

1928 The television station W2XBS is established in New York by the Radio Corporation of America (RCA). It begins testing by transmitting an image of a Felix the Cat toy.

1929 The state-run British Broadcasting Corporation (BBC) begins experimental television broadcasts in London using a primitive mechanical/electrical system.

1932 Radio broadcasting begins in Nigeria. The first such program in Africa, it is an arm of the BBC Empire Service (later World Service), which disseminates BBC programming in British colonies.

1937 Germany establishes a fully electronic television system, adopting an image resolution of 441 scan lines, a standard that will extend into Paris in 1941 with German occupation.

1941 In the United States, the National Television Standards Committee (NTSC) stipulates that video should be encoded, transmitted, and received at 525 lines and a speed of thirty frames per second, a rate compatible with the country's 60 Hz power system.

1944 The Soviet Union standardizes television broadcasting at 625 lines and a speed of twenty-five frames per second (compatible with the USSR's 50 Hz power system).

1946 Experimental television broadcasts begin in Cuba and Mexico City, building on established radio networks.

1948 Compelled by the use of the Soviet standard in East Germany, West Germany adopts a 625-line television standard, allowing for communication between East and West throughout the Cold War. Austria, Belgium, Denmark, Italy, the Netherlands, Sweden, and Switzerland also adopt the standard, while Britain retains its prewar 405-line system and France uses a 819-line system.

Entrepreneurs in the United States begin retransmitting commercial television broadcasts via cable to nearby communities with poor reception to over-the-air signals. Television broadcasting is mainly confined to northeastern metropolitan cities.

1950 Commercial television stations begin broadcasting in Mexico City and Brazil.

1951 President Harry S. Truman addresses the nation in the first coast-to-coast television broadcast in the United States.

1953 The NTSC codifies the addition of color to the television signal. Saturation and hue must be manually adjusted on the TV set, and the standard gains the nickname "Never the Same Color."

With the advent of color TV, television adoption in the United States explodes. Commercial television is dominated by the "big three" networks: NBC, ABC, and CBS, all former radio stations.

Television broadcasting begins in Japan after disruptions caused by World War II.

1956 Western Nigeria Television, the first television station in Africa, is established in cooperation with the London-based company Overseas Rediffusion.

Engineers in France begin developing SECAM (Séquentiel de Couleur à Mémoire), a standard for color television that eliminates the inefficiencies of NTSC. SECAM is eventually adopted in the Soviet Union and France and forced on France's former colonies on the west coast of Africa.

The Quadruplex video tape recorder (VTR), by Ampex, allows for instant playback of recorded audio and video, eliminating the time lag necessitated by earlier, film-based recording technologies.

Television broadcasting is introduced in Australia, with both a government-funded service and commercial stations in operation before the Melbourne Olympic Games that summer.

1959 US vice president Richard Nixon and Soviet premier Nikita Khrushchev debate the merits of their respective economic and political systems in an unscripted exchange at a fair in Moscow. Captured by cameras demonstrating the new American technology of color television, the exchange—known as the Kitchen Debate—is broadcast nationally in the United States the next day and in the Soviet Union three days later.

1962 The Telstar telecommunications satellite is launched. A collaboration by AT&T, NASA, Bell Telephone, the UK's General Post Office, and the French firm National PTT, it broadcasts to stations in the United States, France, the UK, Canada, West Germany, and Italy.

The American All-Channel Receiver Act increases access to the airwaves, paving the way for public broadcasting, the entry of new stations into the market, and, eventually, pirate television.

1963 The Phase Alternating Line (PAL) system is introduced to the European Broadcasting Union. This standard for transmitting television in color (similar to SECAM) is adopted over much of Western Europe, but not in France, East Germany, or the Soviet Union.

1964 The Brazilian military regime subsidizes television sets for the populace and partners with the television network Globo to create programming and provide satellite access.

The Tokyo Olympic Games are broadcast worldwide via a satellite system developed by Japan.

1967 The Sony Portapak is released in the US market. Unlike earlier video equipment, the battery-operated commercial camcorder can be carried and operated by a single person.

Nearly 90 percent of American households have at least one television receiver.

Our World, the first multinational, multi-satellite live television production, is broadcast simultaneously in twenty-four countries. The two-hour program reaches an estimated audience of 500 million viewers.

1969 A computer link established between UCLA and the Stanford Research Institute marks the inauguration of the ARPANET. Organized by the US Department of Defense, the novel computer network allows for electronic communication among users at various universities.

1971 Sony launches U-matic, a cassette-based video format, making the medium easier and cheaper to work with. Filmmakers and artists quickly adopt U-matic in production, postproduction, and exhibition, and the video art and guerrilla documentary scenes explode.

1972 In the United States, the Federal Communications Commission relaxes its regulation of cable television, allowing for the importation of non-local signals and the growth of original networks and channels. The United States' first pay-TV cable network, Home Box Office (HBO), is launched.

1973 The CVS 502, the first stand-alone time base corrector (TBC), brings material recorded with Portapak cameras and U-matic videocassettes to broadcast standard, enabling artists and other amateur video users to circulate their work to a wider audience.

1976 JVC releases the Video Home System (VHS), introducing recorded video into the home via videocassettes and VTRs designed for the consumer market.

1981 The International Radio Consultative Committee (CCIR) develops a standard for encoding analog video into a digital format, stipulating a resolution of 486 lines.

India launches the Ariane Passenger PayLoad Experiment (APPLE), its first telecommunications satellite.

1984 A working group of the Society of Motion Picture and Television Engineers proposes a 16:9 aspect ratio for high-definition (HD) video—an average of the most popular existing ratios, including the 4:3 standard television ratio.

China launches its first telecommunications satellite, making possible the dissemination of central-government programming in remote areas such as Tibet and Xinjiang.

1987 Video Graphics Array (VGA), introduced in a line of IBM computers, allows for the on-screen display of digital photographic images.

1988 The International Telecommunication Union (ITU) releases the first digital video compression standard.

1989 Employed by the Conseil Européen pour la Recherche Nucléaire (CERN), Tim Berners-Lee develops the World Wide Web, an electronic information system designed to facilitate automated sharing among scientists around the world.

With developments in satellite and cable broadcasting, state-controlled television broadcast models in many countries begin to give way to a commercial model of private ownership like that of the United States.

1990 In reunified Germany, the former East switches from the SECAM standard to PAL. The development of private, commercial stations signals a move away from state-regulated television.

1993 The CCIR increases the resolution of HD video to a maximum of 1,080 lines, effectively doubling it.

Scientists in the Computer Laboratory at the University of Cambridge broadcast live video of their shared coffeepot over the World Wide Web, creating the first streaming webcam.

1994 The ITU and the Motion Picture Experts Group, an international alliance of experts, jointly develop the MPEG-2 encoding standard for digital video. It is adopted for digital video discs (DVDs), which are released a few years later, replacing VHS tapes as the most popular consumer format for standard-definition video.

1995 Sony releases the first DV camcorder. DV gains popularity among amateurs and professionals, becoming the dominant consumer digital video format. Editing software such as Final Cut Pro and iMovie make video postproduction accessible to the consumer.

A baseball game between the Seattle Mariners and the New York Yankees is live streamed on the internet. ESPNET's SportsZone digitally transmits the live radio broadcast, making it accessible anywhere in the world.

1996 Using new plasma and liquid crystal diode (LCD) technology, Sony and Sharp develop a large, flat-screen television monitor.

1998 The MPEG-4 encoding standard delivers higher resolution—up to four thousand (4K) lines—and support for digital rights management.

In the United States, the Digital Millennium Copyright Act criminalizes the circumvention of measures controlling access to copyrighted material and increases penalties for copyright infringement on the internet.

2001 The BitTorrent protocol speeds up file transfers over peer-to-peer networks on the internet, allowing users to easily share and access large movie and music files free of charge.

Video conferencing is introduced in America Online's Instant Messenger and other chat services.

2005 The video-sharing website YouTube launches in May. By the following January, it is receiving more than twenty-five million views per day.

2007 Building on its mail-based DVD subscription service, Netflix begins streaming movies and television series, bringing video-on-demand to the internet.

Viacom, the corporate parent of CBS, sues YouTube over copyright infringement, demanding $1 billion in damages. The suit is settled seven years later.

2009 Two years after the launch of the iPhone, Apple releases the iPhone 3GS, the first model with video-recording capacity.

Analog television transmission in the United States ceases, making cathode-ray-tube televisions obsolete and establishing 16:9 as the dominant aspect ratio for video.

2010 Video conferencing via FaceTime is introduced in the iPhone 4.

2011 Antigovernment protests erupt in Tunisia. Protesters use social media such as YouTube and Facebook to broadcast video of the uprisings and reprisals, and unrest spreads through the Middle East and North Africa, galvanizing the Arab Spring.

2016 The manufacture of analog videotape largely ceases.

The social-media app TikTok begins hosting and disseminating short-form videos, serving its millions of users with content selected by an artificial-intelligence algorithm.

2020 The popularity of video conferencing and video chat (via applications such as Zoom, Google Hangouts, and Cisco Webex) skyrockets around the world, spurred by the COVID-19 pandemic.

2022 The term "TikTok war" is coined to refer to the massive transmission and dissemination of video footage, information, and misinformation about the Russian invasion of Ukraine on the app.

Streaming services claim the largest share of television viewing in the United States, surpassing both cable and broadcast television.

Research compiled by PETER OLEKSIK

Checklist of the Exhibition

Lawrence Abu Hamdan
Walled Unwalled. 2018
High-definition video (color, sound), 20:04 min.
The Museum of Modern Art, New York. Acquired through the generosity of Elie Khouri [Pages 162–65]

Ant Farm
(USA, founded 1968)
Media Burn. 1975–2003
Standard-definition video (color, sound), 23:02 min.
The Museum of Modern Art, New York. Acquired through the generosity of Celeste Bartos and as a gift of Chip Lord [Page 20]

American Artist
(American, born 1989)
2015. 2019
High-definition video (color, sound), 21:56 min.
The Museum of Modern Art, New York. Fund for the Twenty-First Century [Pages 32, 33]

American Artist
(American, born 1989)
Untitled. 2019
Curtains and bleachers, dimensions variable
The Museum of Modern Art, New York. Fund for the Twenty-First Century

Liza Béar
(British, born 1942)
Keith Sonnier
(American, 1941–2020)
Send/Receive I and *Send/Receive II*. 1977
Standard-definition video (color, sound), 61:40 min.
Video Data Bank, School of the Art Institute of Chicago

Gretchen Bender
(American, 1951–2004)
TV Text and Image (Donnell Library Center Version). 1990
Live television broadcast on twelve cathode-ray-tube monitors, vinyl lettering, and shelves, dimensions variable
The Museum of Modern Art, New York. Acquired through the generosity of Jill and Peter Kraus [Pages 124–27]

Dara Birnbaum
(American, born 1946)
Tiananmen Square: Break-In Transmission. 1990
Five-channel standard-definition video installation (color, four-channel stereo sound; various durations), surveillance switcher, and custom hardware, dimensions variable
Courtesy the artist and Marian Goodman Gallery [Pages 25, 26]

Black Audio Film Collective
(UK, active 1982–1998)
John Akomfrah
(British, born 1957)
Handsworth Songs. 1986
16mm film transferred to high-definition video (color, sound), 58:33 min.
Courtesy Smoking Dogs Films and Lisson Gallery [Pages 30, 39, 82–83]

CADA (Colectivo Acciones de Arte)
(Chile, active 1979–1985)
¡Ay Sudamérica! (Oh, South America!). 1981
Standard-definition video (black and white and color, sound), 12 min.
The Museum of Modern Art, New York. Gift of the artists [Pages 70–73]

Peter Callas
(Australian, born 1952)
NEO-GEO: An American Purchase. 1989
Standard-definition video (color, sound), 9:17 min.
The Museum of Modern Art, New York. Acquired through the generosity of The Contemporary Arts Council of The Museum of Modern Art

Chto Delat
(Russia, founded 2003)
The Excluded. In a Moment of Danger. 2014
Four-channel high-definition video (color, sound), 56:46 min.
The Museum of Modern Art, New York. Fund for the Twenty-First Century [Pages 152–55]

Tony Cokes
(American, born 1956)
Black Celebration. 1988
Standard-definition video (black and white, sound), 17:11 min.
The Museum of Modern Art, New York. Friends of Education and Committee on Media and Performance Funds [Pages 18, 36, 41, 84–87]

David Cort
(American, 1935–2020)
Mayday Realtime. 1971
Standard-definition video (black and white, sound), 59:45 min.
The Museum of Modern Art, New York. Purchase

Jaime Davidovich
(American, born Argentina. 1936–2016)
QUBE Project. 1980
Standard-definition video (color, sound), 10:32 min.
Electronic Arts Intermix (EAI), New York

Jaime Davidovich
(American, born Argentina. 1936–2016)
The Live! Show Promo. 1982
Standard-definition video (color, sound), 5:32 min.
Electronic Arts Intermix (EAI), New York

Jaime Davidovich
(American, born Argentina. 1936–2016)
The Live! Show (April 29, 1983). 1983
Standard-definition video (color, sound), 27 min.
Electronic Arts Intermix (EAI), New York

VALIE EXPORT
(Austrian, born 1940)
Body Politics. 1974
Standard-definition video (black and white, sound), 2:16 min.
The Museum of Modern Art, New York. Gift of VALIE EXPORT and Miryam and Daniel Charim

Harun Farocki
(German, 1944–2014)
Andrei Ujică
(Romanian, born 1951)
Videograms of a Revolution. 1992
16mm film transferred to standard-definition video (color, sound), 106 min.
The Museum of Modern Art, New York. Given anonymously in honor of Anna Marie Shapiro [Pages 22, 27, 29]

Regina José Galindo
(Guatemalan, born 1974)
America's Family Prison. 2008
Standard-definition video (color, silent), 54:49 min.
The Museum of Modern Art, New York. Gift of Patricia Phelps de Cisneros through the Latin American and Caribbean Fund in honor of Agnes Gund and The Art for Justice Fund

Kit Galloway
(American, born 1948)
Sherrie Rabinowitz
(American, 1950–2013)
Hole in Space. 1980
Recording of a life-size, interactive, and telecollaborative public video/audio satellite link connecting pedestrians in Los Angeles and New York for three days. Two-channel standard-definition video (black and white, sound), 60 min.
Sherrie Rabinowitz and Kit Galloway Archives [Pages 6–7]

Kit Galloway
(American, born 1948)
Sherrie Rabinowitz
(American, 1950–2013)
Hole in Space: A Public Communication Sculpture. 1980
Standard-definition video (black and white, sound), 30 min.
The Museum of Modern Art, New York. Purchase

Anna Bella Geiger
(Brazilian, born 1933)
Passagens 1 (Passages 1). 1974
Standard-definition video (black and white, sound), 9:55 min.
The Museum of Modern Art, New York. Purchase

General Idea
(Canada, active 1969–1994)
Test Tube. 1979
Standard-definition video (color, sound), 28:15 min.
The Museum of Modern Art, New York. Purchase [Pages 66–69]

Frank Gillette
(American, born 1941)
Ira Schneider
(American, 1939–2022)
Wipe Cycle. 1969/2022
Two standard-definition videos (black and white, silent; 14 min.); sound; live television broadcast; surveillance camera; nine cathode-ray-tube monitors; custom video switcher, microcontrollers, and software; and shelving, overall (approx.): 7' 10 1/2" × 6' 10 11/16" × 29 9/16" (240 × 210 × 75 cm)
Courtesy Frank Gillette and Estate of Ira J. Schneider. Reconstruction: Daniel Heiss, ZKM | Center for Art and Media Karlsruhe

Dan Graham
(American, 1942–2022)
Performer/Audience/Mirror. 1975
Standard-definition video (black and white, sound), 22:52 min.
The Museum of Modern Art, New York. Gift of Jerry I. Speyer and Katherine G. Farley, Anna Marie and Robert F. Shapiro, and Marie-Josée and Henry R. Kravis

Mona Hatoum
(British-Palestinian, born 1952)
Measures of Distance. 1988
Standard-definition video (color, sound), 15:26 min.
The Museum of Modern Art, New York. Purchase [Pages 122–23]

Every Ocean Hughes
(American, born 1977)
Sense and Sense. 2010
Two-channel high-definition video (color, silent), 15:25 min.
The Museum of Modern Art, New York. Fund for the Twenty-First Century

Mako Idemitsu
(Japanese, born 1940)
Another Day of a Housewife. 1977–78
Standard-definition video (color, sound), 18 min.
The Museum of Modern Art, New York. Gift of the artist

Sanja Iveković
(Croatian, born 1949)
Osobni rezovi (Personal Cuts). 1982
Standard-definition video (color, sound), 4 min.
The Museum of Modern Art, New York. Gift of Jerry I. Speyer and Katherine G. Farley, Anna Marie and Robert F. Shapiro, Marie-Josée and Henry R. Kravis, and Committee on Media and Performance Art Funds

Emily Jacir
(American, born 1970)
Ramallah/New York. 2004–05
Two-channel standard-definition video (color, sound; 38:50 min.) and two flat-screen monitors, dimensions variable
The Museum of Modern Art, New York. Fund for the Twenty-First Century

Ulysses Jenkins
(American, born 1946)
Mass of Images. 1978
Standard-definition video (black and white, sound), 4:19 min.
Electronic Arts Intermix (EAI), New York

Amar Kanwar
(Indian, born 1964)
The Torn First Pages. 2004–08
Nineteen-channel standard-definition video (black and white and color, sound and silent; varying durations), nineteen sheets of paper, three metal frames, books, magazines, and artist books, dimensions variable
The Museum of Modern Art, New York. Acquired through the generosity of The Estate of Byron R. Meyer, Kiran Nadar of Kiran Nadar Museum of Art, and The Contemporary Arts Council [Pages 111, 142–45]

Dana Kavelina
(Ukrainian, born 1995)
Letter to a Turtledove. 2020
High-definition video (color, sound), 20:55 min.
The Museum of Modern Art, New York. Acquired through the generosity of Bilge Ogut and Haro Cumbusyan [Pages 18, 166–69]

Michael Klier
Der Riese (The Giant). 1983
Standard-definition video (black and white and color, sound), 82 min.
The Museum of Modern Art, New York. Committee on Media and Performance Funds [Page 19]

Lynn Hershman Leeson
(American, born 1941)
Seduction of a Cyborg. 1994
Standard-definition video
(color, sound), 7 min.
The Museum of Modern Art, New
York. The Modern Women's Fund

Carlos Leppe
(Chilean, 1952–2015)
Acción de la estrella
(*Star Action*). 1979
Standard-definition video
(color, sound), 20 min.
The Museum of Modern Art, New York.
Gift of Pedro Montes through the
Latin American and Caribbean Fund

Victor Masayesva Jr.
(Native American, born 1951)
Ritual Clowns. 1988
Standard-definition video
(color, sound), 18 min.
The Museum of Modern Art,
New York. Purchase [Pages 118–21]

Marta Minujín
(Argentine, born 1943)
Simultaneidad en simultaneidad
(*Simultaneity in Simultaneity*). 1966
Documents, slides, and ephemera,
dimensions variable
The Museum of Modern Art, New
York. Promised gift of the Institute
for Studies on Latin American Art
(ISLAA), New York [Pages 46–49]

Carlos Motta
(Colombian, born 1978)
Shape of Freedom: Triangle. 2012
Synthetic polymer paint and
mirror on wood, and audio, overall:
8 1/2″ × 14′ 11″ (21.6 × 454.6 cm).
Voice narration: Ari Shapiro
The Museum of Modern Art,
New York. Gift of Filomena Soares
and Manuel Santos [Page 148]

Carlos Motta
(Colombian, born 1978)
We Who Feel Differently. 2012
Custom platforms and seating,
carpet, five-channel high-definition
video (color, sound; varying durations),
five custom LCD monitors, desktop
computer, website, six sets of
headphones, inkjet print mounted on
wood, four inkjet prints on paper, and
vinyl lettering, dimensions variable
The Museum of Modern Art, New York.
Acquired through the generosity
of The David Sanders Living Trust,
Pedro Barbosa, Mrs. Clarice Tavaras,
TPCA Collection-Thibault Poutrel,
and Steven Johnson [Pages 146–49]

Sandra Mujinga
(Norwegian, born Congo 1989)
Flo. 2019
High-definition video (color, sound;
50:13 min.), polycarbonate plate, MDF,
and wood beams, dimensions variable
The Museum of Modern Art, New York.
Fund for the Twenty-First Century

Sandra Mujinga
(Norwegian, born Congo 1989)
Pervasive Light. 2021
Three-channel high-definition
video (color, sound; 16:15 min.)
and three flat-screen monitors,
dimensions variable. Performed
by Mariama Ndure. Camera: Andre
Katombe. Music: NaEE RoBErts
The Museum of Modern Art, New York.
Fund for the Twenty-First Century
[Pages 170–71]

Muntadas
(Spanish, born 1942)
Marshall Reese
(American, born 1955)
*Political Advertisement X:
1952–2020*. 2020
Standard-definition video (black
and white and color, sound), 92 min.
Electronic Arts Intermix (EAI), New York

Fujiko Nakaya
(Japanese, born 1933)
*Friends of Minamata Victims—
Video Diary*. 1972
Standard-definition video (black
and white, sound), 20 min.
The Museum of Modern Art, New York.
Gift of the artist [Pages 58–61]

New Red Order
(formation c. 2016, ongoing)
*Culture Capture: Crimes against
Reality*. 2020
Two-channel high-definition
video (color, sound), 9 min.
The Museum of Modern Art, New York.
Fund for the Twenty-First Century

Not Channel Zero
(USA, active 1990s)
Not Channel Zero Goes to War. 1992
Standard-definition video
(color, sound), 30 min.
Courtesy the artists, distributed
by Third World Newsreel

Nam June Paik
(American, born Korea. 1932–2006)
Electronic Opera #1. 1969
Segment from the GBH production
*New Television Workshop: The Medium
Is the Medium*. Standard-definition
video (color, sound), 4:45 min.
GBH Archives [Pages 91, 97]

Nam June Paik
(American, born Korea. 1932–2006)
Bonjour, M. Orwell. 1984
Standard-definition video
(color, sound), 57:59 min.
Long Beach Museum of Art Video
Archive, Research Library, The Getty
Research Institute. Transferred
by the Long Beach Museum of Art
Foundation and the City of Long
Beach, 2005

Nam June Paik
(American, born Korea. 1932–2006)
Good Morning, Mr. Orwell. 1984
Standard-definition video
(color, sound), 38 min.
Edited by Skip Blumberg
The Museum of Modern Art,
New York. Gift of the artist
[Pages 74–77, 95, 96]

Nam June Paik
(American, born Korea. 1932–2006)
Good Morning, Mr. Orwell. 1984
Standard-definition video
(color, sound), 48 min.
Electronic Arts Intermix
(EAI), New York

Nam June Paik
(American, born Korea. 1932–2006)
Good Morning, Mr. Orwell. 1984
Standard-definition video
(color, sound), 60 min.
Long Beach Museum of Art Video
Archive, Research Library, The Getty
Research Institute. Transferred
by the Long Beach Museum
of Art Foundation and the City
of Long Beach, 2005

Nam June Paik
(American, born Korea. 1932–2006)
Jud Yalkut
(American, 1938–2013)
Video Tape Study No. 3. 1967–69/1992
Standard-definition video (black
and white, sound), 4:01 min.
The Museum of Modern Art,
New York. Acquired through
the generosity of Barbara Wise
[Page 88]

Letícia Parente
(Brazilian, 1930–1991)
Preparação I (*Preparation I*). 1975
Standard-definition video (black
and white, sound), 3:31 min.
The Museum of Modern Art,
New York. Latin American
and Caribbean Fund

Sondra Perry
(American, born 1986)
Double Quadruple Etcetera Etcetera I & II. 2013
Two-channel high-definition video (color, silent), 9 min.
The Museum of Modern Art, New York. Acquired through the generosity of Lonti Ebers, Sarah Arison, The Lumpkin-Boccuzzi Family Collection, and The Modern Women's Fund [Pages 18, 150–51]

Howardena Pindell
(American, born 1943)
Free, White and 21. 1980
Standard-definition video (color, sound), 12:15 min.
The Museum of Modern Art, New York. Gift of Jerry I. Speyer and Katherine G. Farley, Anna Marie and Robert F. Shapiro, and Marie-Josée and Henry R. Kravis

Walid Raad
(Lebanese, born 1967)
Souheil Bachar
Hostage: The Bachar Tapes (English Version). 2001
Standard-definition video (color, sound), 16:17 min.
The Museum of Modern Art, New York. Gift of the Jerome Foundation in honor of its founder, Jerome Hill [Pages 136–37]

Raindance Corporation
(USA, founded 1969)
Proto Media Primer. 1970
Standard-definition video (black and white, sound), 16:05 min.
Electronic Arts Intermix (EAI), New York [Pages 50, 51, 53]

Raindance Corporation
(USA, founded 1969)
Media Primer (Shamberg). 1971
Standard-definition video (black and white, sound), 16:29 min.
Electronic Arts Intermix (EAI), New York [Pages 50–53]

Marlon Riggs
(American, 1957–1994)
Anthem. 1991
Standard-definition video (black and white and color, sound), 9 min.
The Museum of Modern Art, New York. Gift of Jerry I. Speyer and Katherine G. Farley, Anna Marie and Robert F. Shapiro, and Marie-Josée and Henry R. Kravis [Pages 128–31]

Martha Rosler
(American, born 1943)
If It's Too Bad to Be True, It Could Be DISINFORMATION. 1985
Standard-definition video (color, sound), 16:26 min.
The Museum of Modern Art, New York. Gift of the artist and Galerie Nagel, Berlin [Pages 78–81]

Eder Santos
(Brazilian, born 1960)
Essa coisa nervosa (This Nervous Thing). 1991
Standard-definition video (color, sound), 15:26 min.
The Museum of Modern Art, New York. Gift of the artist

Julia Scher
(American, born 1954)
Information America. 1995
Metal office desk, five closed-circuit cathode-ray-tube monitors with metal wall brackets, one color cathode-ray-tube monitor, plastic and vinyl signage, three black-and-white surveillance cameras, removable lenses, transformers, video matrix switchers, two time-lapse recorders, Amiga A1200HD computer, Sony Watch-Cam, two media players, desk lamp, office chair, wires, and cables, dimensions variable
The Museum of Modern Art, New York. The Jill and Peter Kraus Media and Performance Acquisition Fund

Richard Serra
(American, born 1938)
Carlota Fay Schoolman
(American, born 1949)
Television Delivers People. 1973
Standard-definition video (color, sound), 6 min.
The Museum of Modern Art, New York. Acquired through the generosity of Barbara Pine [Pages 16, 62–65]

Tiffany Sia
(American, born Hong Kong 1988)
Never Rest/Unrest. 2020
High-definition video (color, sound), 29 min.
The Museum of Modern Art, New York. Fund for the Twenty-First Century [Pages 19, 100–107]

Song Dong
(Chinese, born 1966)
Broken Mirror. 1999
Standard-definition video (color, sound), 3:54 min.
The Museum of Modern Art, New York. Committee on Media and Performance Art Funds [Pages 132–35]

Frances Stark
(American, born 1967)
U.S. Greatest Hits Mix Tape Volume I: Afghanistan 1979. 2019
Standard-definition video (color, sound; 3:07 min.); iPad, lightning-to-USB power cable, electrical cord, ribbon, twine, cutout wood numbers, and paper on board; electrical tape and marker, 16 1/8 × 20 1/16 × 1 9/16″ (41 × 51 × 4 cm)
The Museum of Modern Art, New York. Promised gift of Jolie Nahigian and van Moskowitz

Frances Stark
(American, born 1967)
U.S. Greatest Hits Mix Tape Volume I: Iran 1953. 2019
High-definition video (color, sound; 3 min.); iPad, lightning-to-USB power cable, electrical cord, ribbon, twine, rope, cutout wood numbers, and paper on board; electrical tape and marker, 24 × 18 1/8 × 1 9/16″ (61 × 46 × 4 cm)
The Museum of Modern Art, New York. Promised gift of Jolie Nahigian and Ivan Moskowitz

Frances Stark
(American, born 1967)
U.S. Greatest Hits Mix Tape Volume I: Libya 2011. 2019
High-definition video (color, sound; 4:05 min.); iPad, lightning-to-USB power cable, electrical cord, ribbon, string with metal stars, cutout wood numbers, and paper on board; electrical tape and marker, 24 × 18 1/8 × 1 9/16″ (61 × 46 × 4 cm)
The Museum of Modern Art, New York. Promised gift of Jolie Nahigian and Ivan Moskowitz

Frances Stark
(American, born 1967)
*U.S. Greatest Hits Mix Tape
Volume I: Syria 1949*. 2019
High-definition video (color,
sound; 2:51 min.); iPad, lightning-
to-USB power cable, electrical
cord, bells, ribbon, twine, cutout
wood numbers, and paper
on board; electrical tape and
marker, 20 1/16 × 16 1/8 × 1 9/16″
(51 × 41 × 4 cm)
The Museum of Modern Art,
New York. Promised gift of Jolie
Nahigian and Ivan Moskowitz

Frances Stark
(American, born 1967)
*U.S. Greatest Hits Mix Tape
Volume I: Ukraine 2013*. 2019
High-definition video (color, sound;
4:06 min.); iPad, lightning-to-USB
power cable, electrical cord, ribbon,
string with metal stars, cutout
wood numbers, and paper on
board; electrical tape and marker,
18 1/8 × 24 × 1 9/16″ (46 × 61 × 4 cm)
The Museum of Modern Art,
New York. Promised gift of Jolie
Nahigian and Ivan Moskowitz

Frances Stark
(American, born 1967)
*U.S. Greatest Hits Mix Tape
Volume I: Venezuela 2019*. 2019
High-definition video (color, sound;
4:06 min.); iPad, lightning-to-USB
power cable, electrical cord, ribbon,
cutout wood numbers, and paper
on board; electrical tape and marker,
24 × 18 1/8 × 1 9/16″ (61 × 46 × 4 cm)
The Museum of Modern Art,
New York. Promised gift of Jolie
Nahigian and Ivan Moskowitz

Martine Syms
(American, born 1988)
Lessons I–CLXXX. 2014–18
180 standard- and high-definition
videos (color, sound), 90 min.
(30 sec. each)
The Museum of Modern Art,
New York. Fund for the Twenty-
First Century [Pages 158–61]

Martine Syms
(American, born 1988)
GIRRRLGIRLLLGGGIRLGIIIRL. 2017
Wall painting, dimensions variable
The Museum of Modern Art,
New York. Fund for the Twenty-
First Century [Page 161]

Rea Tajiri
(American, born 1958)
History and Memory. 1991
Standard-definition video (black
and white and color, sound), 32 min.
The Museum of Modern Art,
New York. Purchase

Marcelo Tas
(Brazilian, born 1959)
Fernando Meirelles
(Brazilian, born 1955)
Varela in Serra Pelada. 1984
Standard-definition video
(color, sound), 20 min.
The Museum of Modern Art,
New York. Purchase

Wu Tsang
(American, born 1982)
The Shape of a Right Statement. 2008
High-definition video (color, sound), 5 min.
The Museum of Modern Art,
New York. Committee on Media
and Performance Art Funds

TVTV
(USA, active 1972–1979)
Four More Years. 1972
Standard-definition video
(black and white, sound), 61:28 min.
The Museum of Modern Art,
New York. Purchase [Pages 54–57]

Stan VanDerBeek
(American, 1927–1984)
Movie-Drome. 1964–65
Dome theater with three 16mm
films (black and white and color,
sound; varying durations), 320 black-
and-white and color 35mm slides,
three 16mm slide projectors, and
sound, dimensions variable
The Museum of Modern Art, New York.
Acquired through the generosity of Jill
and Peter Kraus, and Jerry I. Speyer
and Katherine Farley [Pages 14, 42–45]

Videofreex
(USA, founded 1969)
*Fred Hampton: Black Panthers
in Chicago*. 1969
Standard-definition video
(black and white, sound), 24 min.
Video Data Bank, School
of the Art Institute of Chicago

Videofreex
(USA, founded 1969)
Money. 1970
Standard-definition video
(black and white, sound), 2:35 min.
Video Data Bank, School
of the Art Institute of Chicago

Videofreex
(USA, founded 1969)
Women's Lib Demonstration NYC. 1970
Standard-definition video (black
and white, sound), 23:30 min.
Video Data Bank, School
of the Art Institute of Chicago

Wolf Vostell
(German, 1932–1998)
Vietnam. 1968–71/1972
Standard-definition video
(black and white, sound), 7:39 min.
The Museum of Modern Art,
New York. Committee on Media
and Performance Art Funds

Ming Wong
(Singaporean, born 1971)
Windows on the World (Part 2). 2014
Twenty-four-channel standard-definition
video (color, sound; varying durations),
twenty-four flat-screen monitors,
MDF, wood, and steel, overall (approx.):
65″ × 13′ 1 1/2″ × 30″ (165 × 400 × 75 cm)
The Museum of Modern Art,
New York. Fund for the Twenty-
First Century [Pages 156–57]

Xu Zhen
(Chinese, born 1977)
Shouting. 1998
Standard-definition video
(color, sound), 3:52 min.
The Museum of Modern Art,
New York. Purchase

Nil Yalter
(Turkish, born Egypt 1938)
Tower of Babel (Immigrants).
1974–77/2016
Eight-channel standard-definition video
(black and white, sound; 20 min.), eight
cathode-ray-tube monitors, and eight
chromogenic color prints on Dibond
and aluminum, dimensions variable
Courtesy the artist

Yau Ching
(Chinese, born 1966)
Flow. 1993
Standard-definition video
(color, sound), 38 min.
The Museum of Modern Art,
New York. Purchase

Artur Żmijewski
(Polish, born 1966)
Democracies. 2009
Twenty-channel high-definition
video (color, sound), 146 min.
The Museum of Modern Art,
New York. Fund for the Twenty-
First Century [Pages 138–41]

Acknowledgments

Video is a fugitive and fluid medium. Defined by its ability to unfold in real time, its capacity for instantaneous dissemination, it has become our virtual, electronic shadow, a parallel system that captures and reshapes the physical world. Reliant on technologies prone to accelerated obsolescence, video is responsive to rapid changes in consumer culture, geopolitics, and the military-industrial complex. To fix for posterity, preservation, and critical analysis such a variable and contingent form can be a daunting challenge, one that has produced a network of invaluable, committed, and pioneering colleagues and collaborators without whom this exhibition would not be possible.

Our profound gratitude to a wide range of colleagues begins with our intrepid curatorial team, who extended incredible care, rigor, and efficiency throughout every step of the process. To Erica Papernik-Shimizu, Lina Kavaliunas, Piper Marshall, Eana Kim, and Rattanamol Singh Johal—we could not be more appreciative of your inspiring commitment to the artists and histories that this show champions. Erica DiBenedetto, Athena Holbrook, Dana Liljegren, Wong Binghao, and Simon Wu also provided essential curatorial support throughout various planning stages of the exhibition.

A media exhibition of this scope and ambition would be unthinkable without the dedication and expertise of our colleagues in the Museum's Conservation and Audio Visual departments. We are deeply grateful for the thoughtful collaboration of Kate Lewis, Chief Conservator, Peter Oleksik, Media Conservator, Amy Brost, Associate Media Conservator, and Aaron Harrow, A/V Design Manager, and their teams. Mack Cole-Edelsack, Associate Director, Exhibition Design and Production, our fundamental partner in devising the thoughtful exhibition design for the show, deserves special acknowledgment.

The writers who contributed to this volume have all been crucial thought partners. We are grateful for the voices of Erika Balsom,

Giampaolo Bianconi, Ina Blom, Aria Dean, Erica DiBenedetto, Jason Dubs, Brandon Eng, Ed Halter, Nina Horisaki-Christens, Marielle Ingram, Danielle A. Jackson, Rattanamol Singh Johal, David Joselit, Inés Katzenstein, Lina Kavaliunas, Inga Lāce, Pamela M. Lee, Glenn Ligon, Peter Oleksik, Oluremi C. Onabanjo, Erica Papernik-Shimizu, Felicity D. Scott, Tiffany Sia, Ravi Sundaram, Lilia Rocio Taboada, Wong Binghao, and Simon Wu.

We were privileged to have a community of international scholars and curators share their time and expertise with us. We gratefully acknowledge the contributions of Carol Brandenburg, Sophie Cavoulacos, Dieter Daniels, Devin Fore, Rudolf Frieling, John G. Hanhardt, May Adadol Ingawanij, William Kaizen, Helen Koh, Barbara London, Ron Magliozzi, Smooth Nzewi, Oluremi C. Onabanjo, Whit Pow, David Ross, Irene Small, David Teh, and Gregory Zinman.

A large family of artists, curators, estates, and representatives provided steady support as we tracked down images and put the pieces together for several works in the show. We are tremendously grateful for the contributions of Suzanne Anker; Miriam Campos-Quinn, Berkeley Art Museum and Pacific Film Archive; Allison Card; Christopher Charles, Yamaguchi Katsuhiro Archive; Michael Connor; Benjamin Cook, LUX; Julia Detchon; Emory Douglas; Diamela Eltit; Peter Friedl; Davidson Gigliotti; Michael Goldberg; Ken Hakuta and Jon Huffman, Nam June Paik Estate; Daniel Heiss and Margit Rosen, ZKM | Center for Art and Media Karlsruhe; Yunsung Hong, Marian Goodman Gallery; Lucy Hunter, Institute for Studies on Latin American Art (ISLAA); Dr. Seong Eun Kim, Chaeyoung Lee, Kwonjin Cho, and Sun Young Kim, Nam June Paik Art Center; Hakudō Kobayashi; Beryl Korot; Barbara Krulik; David Lawson, Smoking Dogs Films; Chip Lord; Mara McCarthy, The Box, Los Angeles; Ryan Muller, Sprüth Magers; Kenta Murakami; Glenn Phillips, Getty Research Institute; Andrew Price and Lotte Parmley, Lisson

Gallery; Allen Rucker; Alison Smith and Lynn Mason, WGBH; Chelsea Spengemann; JT Takagi and Roselly Torres, Third World Newsreel; Sara VanDerBeek; Megan Williams; and Koyo Yamashita.

Video distribution has been the subject of dreams and debates reaching back to the earliest stages of media history. It was our great privilege to build on MoMA's decades-long collaboration with Electronic Arts Intermix (EAI), New York, and Video Data Bank (VDB), Chicago. We are profoundly appreciative of the critical work of Rebecca Cleman and Karl McCool at EAI, Emily Martin at VDB, and their colleagues, who support the ecosystem that provides access to so much of the work that has defined the medium.

Zak Kyes, Florence Meunier, and Belle Place at Zak Group in London more than met the challenge of conceiving a design for this publication that could express video—a form that cannot easily be captured by a single still image—in all of its complexity. We are incredibly grateful for their articulate vision, which brilliantly conveys the energy of the work.

This catalogue's many elements and voices and the robust texts that appear in the exhibition galleries were brought together with unparalleled dedication, patience, and care by MoMA's Publications team: Rebecca Roberts, Dawn Chan, Matthew Pimm, Naomi Falk, Maria Marchenkova, Hannah Kim, Don McMahon, Marc Sapir, and Curtis Scott, with the expert assistance of Craig Rodmore and Xueli Wang.

The online channel for *Signals* is a critical component of the exhibition, and we thank Michelle Pae, Director of Digital Product, Stephanie Schapowal, Digital Product Designer, and Prudence Peiffer, Managing Editor, Creative Team, for their innovative work on this platform.

The support and engagement of Glenn D. Lowry, The David Rockefeller Director; Sarah Suzuki, Associate Director; Kathy Halbreich, former Associate Director; Christy Thompson, Senior Deputy Director, Exhibitions and Collections; Ramona Bannayan, former Senior Deputy Director, Exhibitions and Collections; and James Gara, Chief Operating Officer, have been instrumental to this exhibition. Our colleagues in the Department of Media and Performance and the Department of Painting and Sculpture have, as ever, been a critical source of daily support and inspiration. MoMA's cohort of Chief Curators—Christophe Cherix, Drawings and Prints; Rajendra Roy, Film; Martino Stierli, Architecture and Design; and Ann Temkin, Painting and Sculpture—as well as Clément Chéroux, former Chief Curator of Photography, were a bedrock of intellectual encouragement and dialogue as plans for *Signals* took shape.

Video began primarily as a collective and collaborative enterprise, an ethos we are proud to share with our colleagues at MoMA, whose labor and love for artists form the backbone of this institution and every project it produces. We are deeply thankful for the privilege of delivering this exhibition with such an invaluable community. We thank Elizabeth Henderson, Exhibition Manager, Erik Patton, Director, and Rachel Kim, Associate Director, Exhibition Planning and Administration; Tom Krueger and the team in Art Handling and Preparation; Sarah Primm, Assistant Registrar, Collections; Diana Pan, Chief Technology Officer; Aaron Louis, Mike Gibbons, Travis Kray, Zachary Prewitt, and Jeffrey Enssle, Audio Visual; the Performance and Live Programs team: Lizzie Gorfaine, Kate Scherer, Olivia Rousey, and Kayva Yang; Heidi Hirschl Orley, Assistant Director, Curatorial Affairs; Prudence Peiffer, Alex Halberstadt, Jason Persse, Naeem Douglas, Kevin Ballon, and Claire Corey, Creative Team; Nisa Mackie, Sara Bodinson, Hannah Fagin, Francesca Rosenberg, Arlette Hernandez, and their colleagues in the Department of Learning and Engagement; Amanda Hicks, Sara Beth Walsh, and Jack Spielsinger, Communications and Public Affairs; Rebecca Stokes and Carly McCloskey, Marketing; Michelle Elligott, Chief of Archives, Library, and Research Collections; James Groom, General Counsel, and Ava Childers, Associate General Counsel; the Department of Visitor Engagement, led by Sonya Shrier and William Umana; Tunji Adeniji, Chief Facilities and Safety Officer; the Department of Security, led by Daniel Platt and Tyrone Wyllie; Meagan Johnson, Nora Webb, Anna Luisa Vallifuoco, Meredith Dean, and Madeline Warner, Institutional Giving; Maggie Lyko and Sylvia Renner, Special Programming and Events; Dore Murphy, Director, Membership; Jay Levenson, Director, International Program; and Robert Kastler and Jennifer Sellar, Imaging and Visual Resources.

MoMA's commitment to artists' video was further solidified by the establishment of the Department of Media and Performance in 2006. The previous chief curators of the department—Klaus Biesenbach and Sabine Breitwieser—both played an important role in building the collection and expanding the range of artists and approaches represented. Their legacy continues as part of *Signals*'s DNA.

MoMA's Committee on Media and Performance, recently chaired by Jill Kraus and then by Lonti Ebers, has also been a staunch supporter of an ambitious range of acquisitions and is unfalteringly committed to the challenges of media conservation. We could not be more grateful for its leadership and support of the department's ongoing curatorial vision. We also thank Pamela and Richard Kramlich, founders of the New Art Trust, as well as SFMOMA and Tate, our partners in that pioneering consortium, which has had a profound impact on the establishment of best-practice standards for the field of media conservation. We are proud to have such committed and farseeing colleagues.

In closing, we humbly acknowledge the artists in the exhibition. Truly pathbreaking visionaries, they have provided us with the critical tools to build a new form of media literacy for the digital age, allowing us to find our bearings amid the world's endless stream of signals.

**STUART COMER/
MICHELLE KUO**

Contributors

Erika Balsom is a Reader in Film Studies at King's College London.

Giampaolo Bianconi is Associate Curator of Modern and Contemporary Art at the Art Institute of Chicago.

Ina Blom is Professor in the Department of Philosophy, Classics, History of Art and Ideas at the University of Oslo and Wigeland Visiting Professor in the Department of Art History at the University of Chicago.

Stuart Comer is The Lonti Ebers Chief Curator of Media and Performance at The Museum of Modern Art, New York.

Aria Dean is an artist based in New York.

Erica DiBenedetto is Curatorial Assistant in the Department of Painting and Sculpture at MoMA.

Jason Dubs is Manager of the Mellon-Marron Research Consortium and Research Programs at MoMA.

Brandon Eng is a PhD candidate in art history at the Institute of Fine Arts, New York University, and a former Mellon-Marron Research Consortium Fellow in the Department of Media and Performance at MoMA.

Ed Halter is a critic and curator based in New York and a founder and director of Light Industry, Brooklyn.

Nina Horisaki-Christens is a Mary Griggs Burke Postdoctoral Teaching Fellow in the Department of Art History and Archaeology at Columbia University.

Marielle Ingram is a writer and filmmaker and a PhD student in the Department of Art History and Archaeology at Columbia University.

Danielle A. Jackson is Curator at Artists Space, New York.

Rattanamol Singh Johal is Assistant Director of the International Program at MoMA and a former Mellon-Marron Research Consortium Fellow in the Department of Painting and Sculpture.

David Joselit is Arthur Kingsley Porter Professor and Chair of the Department of Art, Film, and Visual Studies at Harvard University.

Inés Katzenstein is Curator of Latin American Art and Director of the Patricia Phelps de Cisneros Research Institute at MoMA.

Lina Kavaliunas is Curatorial Assistant in the Department of Painting and Sculpture at MoMA.

Michelle Kuo is The Marlene Hess Curator of Painting and Sculpture at MoMA.

Inga Lāce is Contemporary and Modern Art Perspectives (C-MAP) Central and Eastern Europe Fellow at MoMA.

Pamela M. Lee is the Carnegie Professor of Modern and Contemporary Art in the Department of the History of Art at Yale University.

Glenn Ligon is an artist based in New York.

Peter Oleksik is Media Conservator at MoMA.

Oluremi C. Onabanjo is Associate Curator in the Department of Photography at MoMA.

Erica Papernik-Shimizu is Associate Curator in the Department of Media and Performance at MoMA.

Felicity D. Scott is Professor of Architecture, Director of the PhD program in Architecture (History and Theory), and Co-director of the program in Critical, Curatorial and Conceptual Practices in Architecture (CCCP) at the Graduate School of Architecture, Planning and Preservation at Columbia University.

Tiffany Sia is an artist, filmmaker, and writer based in New York.

Ravi Sundaram is Professor and Co-director of the Sarai media program at the Centre for the Study of Developing Societies (CSDS), Delhi.

Lilia Rocio Taboada is Curatorial Assistant in the Department of Media and Performance at MoMA.

Wong Binghao is Contemporary and Modern Art Perspectives (C-MAP) Asia Fellow at MoMA.

Simon Wu is a writer and curator. He is Program Coordinator for the Racial Imaginary Institute and a PhD student in the Department of the History of Art at Yale University.

Photograph Credits

In reproducing the images contained in this publication, the Museum obtained the permission of the rights holders whenever possible. If the Museum could not locate the rights holders, notwithstanding good-faith efforts, it requests that any contact information concerning such rights holders be forwarded so that they may be contacted for future editions.

Works by the following artists are © 2023 by the artist or their estate: Lawrence Abu Hamdan, Ant Farm, American Artist, Gretchen Bender, Dara Birnbaum, CADA (Colectivo Acciones de Arte), CAMP, Chto Delat, Tony Cokes, Peter Friedl, General Idea, Mona Hatoum, Amar Kanwar, Dana Kavelina, Michael Klier, Victor Masayesva Jr., Marta Minujín, Carlos Motta, Rabih Mroué, Sandra Mujinga, Fujiko Nakaya, Nam June Paik, Sondra Perry, Walid Raad, Raindance Corporation, Raqs Media Collective, Marlon Riggs, Martha Rosler, Tiffany Sia, Song Dong, TVTV, Stan VanDerBeek, Ming Wong, Artur Żmijewski.

Courtesy Lawrence Abu Hamdan and Sfeir-Semler Gallery, Beirut/Hamburg: 164 (bottom). © 2023 John Akomfrah/Smoking Dogs Films/Black Audio Film Collective, courtesy Smoking Dogs Films and Lisson Gallery: 30, 39, 82–83. AP Images/Aijaz Rahi: 115 (fig. 8). Courtesy American Artist and Commonwealth and Council, Los Angeles and Mexico City: 32 (fig. 2), 33. Courtesy Gretchen Bender Estate and Sprüth Magers Gallery: 124–27. Courtesy Dara Birnbaum and Marian Goodman Gallery: 25 (fig. 2), 26; photograph by Thierry Bal: jacket, 25 (fig. 1). Courtesy CAMP: 108, 112–13, 117; photograph by Konstantin Guz: 113 (top and bottom). Courtesy Centre d'Art Contemporain Genève and Maureen Paley, London, photograph by Mathilda Olmi: 163 (bottom), 165 (bottom). Deutsche Press: 99. Cover design © 2023 Emory Douglas/Licensed by AFNYLAW.com: 16 (top). Courtesy Electronic Arts Intermix (EAI), New York: 20,

51–53, 55, 56 (top), 57 (top), 74–77, 88, 95, 96 (fig. 6). © 2023 Harun Farocki Filmproduktion: 22, 27, 29. Courtesy Frameline/Signifyin' Works: 128–31. GBH Archives: 91, 97. Courtesy Davidson Gigliotti and Beryl Korot: 11, 15 (top, left and right). © 2023 Michael Goldberg: 16 (bottom). © Solomon R. Guggenheim Museum, New York, photograph by David Heald: 94; photograph by Mathias Schormann: 111 (fig. 3). © 2023 Joan Jonas/Artists Rights Society (ARS), New York, courtesy Electronic Arts Intermix (EAI), New York: 93. Courtesy Dana Kavelina and Fridman Gallery: 18 (bottom), 166–69. Courtesy The Kitchen Archive, c. 1971–99, the Getty Research Institute, Los Angeles: 96 (fig. 5). Courtesy Hakudō Kobayashi: 17 (top). Photograph by Naho Kubota: 147 (top), 148 (top). Photograph by Chip Lord: 57 (bottom). Courtesy MACBA: 34. Courtesy Marta Minujín Studio and Henrique Faria, New York: 46–49. © montweART, photograph by Manfred Montwé: 98 (fig. 9). The Museum of Modern Art, New York. The Gilbert and Lila Silverman Fluxus Collection Gift: 98 (fig. 8), 99. Digital image © 2023 The Museum of Modern Art, New York, Department of Imaging and Visual Resources: 99; photograph by Denis Doorly: 11; photograph by Robert Gerhardt: 12 (bottom), 15 (top, left and right), 98 (fig. 8); photograph by James Mathews: 12 (top). The Museum of Modern Art Archives, New York: 12 (top and bottom). The Museum of Modern Art Library, New York: 15 (top, left and right). Courtesy New Museum, photograph by Dario Lasagni: 171 (top). © 2023 Northwestern University, photograph by Peter Moore, Peter Moore Photography Archive, Charles Deering McCormick Library of Special Collections, Northwestern University Libraries: 43 (top). Courtesy Maureen Paley, London: 163 (top), 164 (top), 165 (top). Courtesy Sondra Perry and Bridget Donahue, NYC: 18 (center), 150–51. Photograph by Tom Powel Imaging: 143 (bottom). Courtesy Queens

Museum, photograph by Hai Zhang: 32 (fig. 1). Courtesy Sherrie Rabinowitz and Kit Galloway Archives, photograph by Lynn Adler: 6; photograph by Karl Hartig: 7. Courtesy Secession, Vienna, photograph by Oliver Ottenschläger: 153 (top). © 2022 Richard Serra/Artists Rights Society (ARS), New York: 16 (center), 62–65. Photograph by Marino Solokhov: 142, 145 (bottom). SRO (Indian Space Research Organization): 13 (bottom). Courtesy Storage by Hyundai Card, 2022, photograph by Byung Cheol Jeon: 161 (top). Courtesy Martine Syms, Sadie Coles HQ, and Bridget Donahue, NYC: 158–61. Photograph by Yuzo Tateishi, *Video Journal*: 17 (bottom). Courtesy Turner Contemporary, Margate, and Maureen Paley, London, photograph by Stephen White: 162. Courtesy TVTV and University of California, Berkeley Art Museum and Pacific Film Archive (BAMPFA): 54, 56 (bottom). Ullstein bild/Granger. All rights reserved: 13 (top). Courtesy Estate of Stan VanDerBeek: 44 (bottom); photograph by Bobby Hansson, courtesy Estate of Bob Hanson: 14 (top), 43 (bottom), 45 (top); photograph by Elliot Landy ©: 45 (bottom); on indefinite loan to MoMA Film Study Center Special Collections: 44 (top, left and right). Courtesy Video Data Bank, School of the Art Institute of Chicago: 122–23, 136–37. Courtesy Ming Wong and Vitamin Creative Space: 156–57. Courtesy Ann Woodward: 10 (top), 14 (bottom).

Major support for this publication is provided by The Museum of Modern Art's Research and Scholarly Publications endowment established through the generosity of The Andrew W. Mellon Foundation, the Edward John Noble Foundation, Mr. and Mrs. Perry R. Bass, and the National Endowment for the Humanities' Challenge Grant Program.

⌐ Hyundai Card ⌐

The exhibition is made possible by Hyundai Card.

Leadership support is provided by the Jill and Peter Kraus Endowed Fund for Contemporary Exhibitions.

Major funding is provided by The International Council of The Museum of Modern Art, the Wallis Annenberg Director's Fund for Innovation in Contemporary Art, and the Thomas H. Lee and Ann Tenenbaum Endowed Fund.

Additional support is provided by the Annual Exhibition Fund. Leadership contributions to the Annual Exhibition Fund, in support of the Museum's collection and collection exhibitions, are generously provided by the Sandra and Tony Tamer Exhibition Fund, Sue and Edgar Wachenheim III, Jerry I. Speyer and Katherine G. Farley, Eva and Glenn Dubin, the Kate W. Cassidy Foundation, Anne Dias, Kenneth C. Griffin, Alice and Tom Tisch, the Marella and Giovanni Agnelli Fund for Exhibitions, Mimi Haas, The David Rockefeller Council, The Contemporary Arts Council of The Museum of Modern Art, Kathy and Richard S. Fuld, Jr., The International Council of The Museum of Modern Art, Marie-Josée and Henry R. Kravis, and Jo Carole and Ronald S. Lauder. Major contributions to the Annual Exhibition Fund are provided by Emily Rauh Pulitzer, The Sundheim Family Foundation, and Karen and Gary Winnick.

Published in conjunction with the exhibition *Signals: How Video Transformed the World*, at The Museum of Modern Art, New York, March 5–July 8, 2023. Organized by Stuart Comer, The Lonti Ebers Chief Curator of Media and Performance, and Michelle Kuo, The Marlene Hess Curator of Painting and Sculpture, with Erica Papernik-Shimizu, Associate Curator, Department of Media and Performance, and Lina Kavaliunas, Curatorial Assistant, Piper Marshall, Exhibition Coordinator, Eana Kim, Marica and Jan Vilcek Fellow, and Rattanamol Singh Johal, Mellon-Marron Research Consortium Fellow, Department of Painting and Sculpture. Thanks to Athena Holbrook, Dana Liljegren, Wong Binghao, and Simon Wu.

Major support for this publication is provided by The Museum of Modern Art's Research and Scholarly Publications endowment established through the generosity of The Andrew W. Mellon Foundation, the Edward John Noble Foundation, Mr. and Mrs. Perry R. Bass, and the National Endowment for the Humanities' Challenge Grant Program.

The exhibition is made possible by Hyundai Card.

Leadership support is provided by the Jill and Peter Kraus Endowed Fund for Contemporary Exhibitions.

Major funding is provided by The International Council of The Museum of Modern Art, the Wallis Annenberg Director's Fund for Innovation in Contemporary Art, and the Thomas H. Lee and Ann Tenenbaum Endowed Fund.

Additional support is provided by the Annual Exhibition Fund. Leadership contributions to the Annual Exhibition Fund, in support of the Museum's collection and collection exhibitions, are generously provided by the Sandra and Tony Tamer Exhibition Fund, Sue and Edgar Wachenheim III, Jerry I. Speyer and Katherine G. Farley, Eva and Glenn Dubin, the Kate W. Cassidy Foundation, Anne Dias, Kenneth C. Griffin, Alice and Tom Tisch, the Marella and Giovanni Agnelli Fund for Exhibitions, Mimi Haas, The David Rockefeller Council, The Contemporary Arts Council of The Museum of Modern Art, Kathy and Richard S. Fuld, Jr., The International Council of The Museum of Modern Art, Marie-Josée and Henry R. Kravis, and Jo Carole and Ronald S. Lauder. Major contributions to the Annual Exhibition Fund are provided by Emily Rauh Pulitzer, The Sundheim Family Foundation, and Karen and Gary Winnick.

Produced by the Department of Publications, The Museum of Modern Art, New York

Hannah Kim, Business and Marketing Director
Don McMahon, Editorial Director
Marc Sapir, Production Director
Curtis R. Scott, Associate Publisher

Edited by Rebecca Roberts and Dawn Chan
Design by Zak Group
Production by Matthew Pimm
Proofread by Craig Rodmore
Printed and bound by Ofset Yapımevi, Istanbul

This book is typeset in True-Sans and ABC Oracle Triple. The paper is 150 gsm Magno Matt and 115 gsm Munken Pure White.

Published by
The Museum of Modern Art
11 West 53 Street
New York, NY 10019-5497
www.moma.org

Library of Congress Control Number: 2022948202
ISBN: 978-1-63345-123-0

Distributed in the United States and Canada by
ARTBOOK | D.A.P.
75 Broad Street
Suite 630
New York, NY 10004
www.artbook.com

Distributed outside the United States and Canada by
Thames & Hudson
181A High Holborn
London WC1V 7QX
www.thamesandhudson.com

Jacket: Dara Birnbaum. *Tiananmen Square: Break-In Transmission.* 1990. Five-channel standard-definition video installation (color, four-channel stereo sound; various durations), surveillance switcher, and custom hardware, dimensions variable. Installation view, Marian Goodman Gallery, London, 2018–19

Printed and bound in Turkey